TAKING CHARGE WITH VALUE INVESTING

HOW TO CHOOSE THE BEST INVESTMENTS ACCORDING TO PRICE, PERFORMANCE, AND VALUATION TO BUILD A WINNING PORTFOLIO

BRIAN NICHOLS

New York   Chicago   San Francisco   Lisbon   London
Madrid   Mexico City   New Delhi   San Juan
Seoul   Singapore   Sydney   Toronto

1 2 3 4 5 6 7 8 9 0   DOC/DOC   1 8 7 6 5 4 3

ISBN   978-0-07-180468-4
MHID   0-07-180468-4

e-ISBN 978-0-7-180469-1
e-MHID   0-07-180469-2

This publication is designed to provide accurate and authoritative information in regard to the subject matter covered. It is sold with the understanding that neither the author nor the publisher is engaged in rendering legal, accounting, or other professional service. If legal advice or other expert assistance is required, the services of a competent professional person should be sought.

— *From a Declaration of Principles Jointly Adopted by a Committee of the American Bar Association and a Committee of Publishers and Associations*

McGraw-Hill books are available at special quantity discounts to use as premiums and sales promotions, or for use in corporate training programs. To contact a representative, please e-mail us at bulksales@mcgraw-hill.com.

This book is printed on acid-free paper.

I dedicate this book to my wife Natalie—for her patience, compassion, and loyalty. She truly is my rock and my much better half. I would also like to dedicate this book to my mother Teresa, my grandmother Deborah, my father Randy, and my mother-in-law Sherrie. But most importantly to my readers—without you none of this would have been possible.

Jeannie Stone who performed the initial read through and helped with the first-line of edits.

Chris Morgan of Morgandesigned.com, continues to show he is one of the best in the industry, designed the cover and all other illustrations.

Contents

Introduction

You never realize the moments that change your outlook on life when they occur. Looking back in my life, there have been many of these moments, but one in particular has really stood out. It occurred when I was a freshman, in a high school economics class, with Mr. Causey, and it really affected my investment strategy and created an intense interest on my part in the industry. Looking back, it was probably my favorite class at any level of education because I found it more useful than any other financial class that I ever took. There were countless lessons and exercises that taught material that I still use today. The class was so instrumental that it helped me find a direction in life. I can recall riding home one day after school and telling my Aunt Becky that I knew what I wanted to do when I finished school—I wanted to work in finance and in the market.

I remember one exercise in particular that allowed me to visualize and understand the basics of a public company. It was the first time that I truly began to understand what drove a public company. The exercise involved our class building its own public company, which included stocks, costs, profits, and real-life operations. In our class, 100 total shares were issued. Each share cost $1, and everyone had to buy at least one share.

As a whole, our class decided to build a company based on candy. We spent $100, which was raised from selling shares, to buy as much candy as possible, leaving some additional cash for unexpected expenses. Over a period of several weeks, the candy was sold at football games, outside events, pageants, and so on, and our goal was to turn our investment into a profit. I can't recall the exact amount of money we earned, but I believe it was near $400. As a result, we divided the $400 into 100 based on the total number of issued shares, which brought our return on investment to $4 on the original $1 we spent for each share. Therefore, in the end, if you purchased 20 shares, your return was $80.

Now here's the catch: When you think of a company or a stock, you need to view it like you would my ninth grade economics project. A stock is a reflection of a company's sales and profits. If a company's earnings increase, its stock should follow suit. There are a lot of factors at play that determine the worth of a company, but when you sort through all the jargon and the various opinions, you'll find that a stock is a reflection of the company's growth, and companies with explosive growth (such as our candy-selling business) might see a higher valuation for growth that exceeds the rate of growth for the industry—all of which will be discussed throughout this book.

We closed the doors of our "business" after only a few weeks and cashed in our stock to live the good life. However, what if we would have continued to operate and reinvested the money into the business? The valuation at the time we "cashed in" was $4 a share, but if we had kept going, how much would you have paid for such a stock? How large could the valuation have become? If we could turn $100 into $400, then how long do we keep this stock, and could we have turned $400 into $1,600? If so, the stock would have been worth $16 a share, and it would have made for a great investment. But would you as an investor maybe have paid a premium for the stock when it was $4 if we would have decided to continue operations? Perhaps an investor, or in this case a 14-year-old student, would have decided that it was worth it to purchase someone else's shares for $6 based on future earnings growth.

These are the types of questions that are answered on a daily basis in the market. For every buyer, there is a seller. And sometimes investors will determine that a stock is worth buying at a premium and will place their bets on the future growth of a company in the hope that a high growth rate can continue. Therefore, if we would have continued our business, it might not have been uncommon for a new investor (or a classmate) to offer $5 to $7 for a share of stock, when it was worth only $4, because of its growth. For argument sake, though, let's play out one more scenario: Would you buy the same shares, valued at $4 a share, if they were priced at $2? Most would say, of course!

You might be thinking, "How could you sell stock in a company at such a discounted price when the earnings growth and fundamentals tell you that it's worth $4?" Fortunately, this occurs every day in the market. The reason it occurs is the same reason that stocks are often bought for premiums—for every buyer, there is a seller, and sometimes the market incorrectly values a company. Sometimes investors may be willing to sell their shares for less because they need quick cash, or maybe they value the company incorrectly. Either way, it can be a gold mine for you if you can correctly identify such a company. So how do you identify when a company is undervalued and is being sold for $2 a share when it's worth $4 or potentially worth even more? How do you find the guts to pull the trigger and buy an underperforming stock but a strong performing company when investors are selling it cheap? And how do you know *when* to buy? In this book, all these questions, plus more, will be answered.

Part I looks at the inner workings of Wall Street and money managers alike. I will explain how the measures of success for you and the firm that handles your money are often few and far between. This includes the fact that firms, such as hedge funds, get paid no matter how your portfolio performs. Most hedge funds use a fee structure that involves earning 2 percent for them on all assets under management and then another 20 percent of annual gains, meaning that they get paid *no matter what*! Throughout the first part of this book, I will explain what this means and also explain how you can perform better by taking charge of your own financial future, which includes developing an economic outlook, separating myths from reality, and introducing value investing in an easy-to-understand manner.

Part II digs deeper into what makes a company a good investment. I will introduce and explain the fundamentals of a company and discuss how a company is valued in the market. This often can be the most confusing aspect of investing, but my goal is to simplify the information and give you a simple way to value a company. This will allow you to make better financial decisions and improve your returns significantly.

Part III looks at the part of investing that has allowed me to become successful: the psychology of the market. By understanding the behavior of the market, you will be better equipped to know when to buy and will understand why stocks may move in an incorrect direction. This will allow you to remain calm and emotionless and return larger gains. In this part I will use life stories and my personal successes and failures as lessons for what to do and what not to do.

Finally, Part IV puts all the information together. I combine the fundamentals with the psychological aspects of the market to find the best stocks. I also will discuss diversification, positioning your portfolio, and how to succeed in the new era of investing.

So let's get started. Sit down next to a fire, have soft piano music playing in the background, grab a notebook, and prepare yourself to change your financial future.

Acknowledgments

Once more, my thanks goes out to my weekly readers who have followed me and have given me the pleasure of helping them to better understand this market. I have learned just as much, if not more, than you have learned from me. We have developed many long-lasting friendships and a unique bond in a cutthroat business world where everyone is out for themselves. If not for you then this book would not exist, and I wouldn't have the honor of spreading our word on an even larger scale. From the absolute bottom of my heart I can't express my sincerity or my gratitude when I say thank you and that it is has been an absolute honor to help and speak with each of you.

While my readers are who made this possible, Seeking Alpha is the company that gave me the platform to write, educate, and then continue to learn more on a daily basis. I am thankful to all the editors that have worked with me and helped me to become a better writer, because back when I first started I had the knowledge but my writing was suspect at best. Mary Hunt and Yosef have always provided so much feedback and pushed me to think outside the box, and constantly prove that they are the absolute best in the industry. And of course no thanks to Seeking Alpha could be complete without mentioning the founder and CEO David Jackson whose knowledge and wisdom is second to none, and pushes others to become better themselves.

Throughout this book I mention on several occasions my experience working for the Department of Corrections at a halfway house. If not for this experience, and my education in psychology, I would not have the mindset that I possess today, as I would view the market in a different light. This was perhaps the most rewarding job I ever had, and although frustrating, the people who both resided and worked at the house were very instrumental in this book, although they don't know, and a special thanks to Paul McNeal, a man that I considered to be more of a mentor or brother than a friend.

Those who know me best will tell you that I am very family oriented, am always loyal to my friends, and have never known a stranger. There are many close friends and family that played a special part in this book, so many that I could never acknowledge everyone. Jeannie Stone, who saw and read it first, spent countless hours making sure that the topics of this book were understandable and readable. I give a most special thank you to Jeannie Stone, a very patient woman who should be acknowledged for the countless hours she spent on this project.

To my oldest friend, Chris Morgan, who participated with all the illustrations and the cover of this book, I say thank you. My mother-in-law, Sherrie Dawahare, also worked on the structure of the book, sometimes without sleep. A huge thank you goes out to these very special people in my life.

Other important thanks include: My mother, who always keeps me grounded and is optimistic regardless of the situation; my grandmother, who has unconditional love and is always faithful regardless of the situation; and my wife, who gives so much more than she takes and is always supportive and pushes me to become a better person. Finally, my agent, Sam Fleishman, and the McGraw-Hill team for bringing this book to life, especially Mary Glenn and Cheryl Ringer.

PART I

CHAPTER 1

Get Prepared

Wall Street is the only place that people ride to in a Rolls
Royce to get advice from those who take the subway.
—WARREN BUFFETT

If you were to ever decide to handle your own finances, you would
find that it just may be the most overly emotional period of your
life. Well, hopefully not the most emotional, but no doubt, it would
definitely rank in the top five. I use the term *overly emotional* because
there is simply not one single emotion that can accurately describe
how someone may feel when he makes a life-changing decision as
such. There are a number of different ways you may feel; you may
feel joyous, excited, or anxious or possibly scared, fearful, or nervous. Either way, emotions run high because it is one of the most
important decisions of your life. It is a decision that very few people
actually entertain but something that everyone is capable of doing.

Your emotions will depend on a variety of factors, such as age,
financial status, career, children, and so on. A 45-year-old man may
view his investments much more differently than a 25-year-old man
and is most likely not willing to take the same risks. The factors

of age, income, and individual responsibilities will determine your thought process and come together to create the volatility of the financial markets.

The stock market is nothing more than a collection of individual people with various goals that all come together yet react in different ways. This would explain why the market acts without reason and why there is no 100 percent proven way to effectively ensure that you "beat" the market 100 percent of the time. Our market acts without reason because it is a place where emotions are at all-time highs because people are trying to protect and increase one of their most valuable assets—money!

In this book my job is to teach you how to invest in equity markets with a logical state of mind and break free from the grasps of professional money managers so that you can take charge of your own financial future. This book is as much about controlling your emotions and understanding the behavior of the market as it is about fundamental knowledge. Knowing how to research and having the ability to understand a company are great, but they are only half the battle. You must understand the market and its tendencies in order to succeed.

TAKE CONTROL

The first step in taking control of your own financial future may be to free yourself of having others control your money. This is a very difficult task for some because the money manager is often a friend or someone you have known for many years. Your money manager is someone you trust and believe to be particularly knowledgeable about investments. In fact, you may think so highly of your money manager that you are unwilling to sacrifice the relationship for a better financial future.

I personally consider myself to be a story teller, and I like to share personal stories that have affected my life. I think personal experiences are sometimes the best way to describe an event or to truly see the meaning or, in this case, insanity of a situation. Such an example can be seen with my friend Tara, who is much older than myself and a person I consider to be very wise in terms of business. She is the perfect example of a person who let the relationship with her financial advisor cloud her ability to make a rational decision. As a result, she is now suffering great financial loss.

Tara, I would say, lives a comfortable life, but she isn't someone I would consider wealthy. She has run a successful chain of fitness centers and has worked hard her entire life. She has used the same financial advisor since she was in her early twenties. Tara and her advisor have developed a close relationship, so Tara trusts this person completely and has remained loyal despite a large loss. I think to fully understand the complexity of the situation, you would have to know Tara. She is the type of person who does not like change and is quite grounded in her decision making.

In 2010, Tara and I discussed her investments, as well as the investment approach of her advisor, while I was visiting another mutual friend. As it was, Tara had lost a very large sum of her total worth during the recession, thanks to her money manager being overweight on financials. She had lost over 40 percent of her portfolio's value, which indicates a lack of diversification on the part of her advisor. She had wanted to talk to me about her financial advisor's plan, which was to invest heavily into the financial sector with index investing. Her financial money manager's logic was similar to that of a lot of the money managers during that time. They felt that the housing crisis had reached its bottom and would recover, positively affecting the banks. Tara, who was somewhat clueless regarding this subject, reluctantly agreed to maintain the plan that she and her advisor had used for so many years, and she believed that this plan could bring her back to even.

The fact that Tara took the time to ask me about and discuss her options showed that she was not very enthusiastic about the chosen strategy her advisor used with her money. She may not have known a lot about investing, but she did know that she had lost a significant amount of her money by investing in the financial system. As a business owner, she was aware of the risks that were still present within the economy. I advised her to seek the opinion of another advisor, but she would not. I also advised her to question her advisor about investing heavier in bonds and other funds, considering her age. Finally, I urged her to consider opening up her own account and allowing me to help educate her regarding her options and how they could help her to save money. She rejected every possible solution, especially if it meant questioning the opinions of her beloved financial manager.

I haven't spoken with Tara for about two years now because my family and I relocated. But if she did not take my advice, which I believe she did not, and she remained quiet, then her portfolio, which was almost all in financials, most likely has declined another 10 percent while the Standard and Poor's 500 Index (S&P 500) has increased over 20 percent within the same time period. Of course, I have no idea what Tara ultimately decided, but I have a strong suspicion that the connection she felt with her advisor blinded her from making rational decisions that must be evaluated when your financial future is at stake.

MONEY MANAGERS ARE LIKE CAR SALESMEN

Tara's dilemma is all too common for a large number of people who let the "professionals" control their portfolio. Some people are very hesitant to confront their advisors about any issues related to their decisions. I have talked with people who are afraid of asking their financial money managers to sell stock because every time they needed money, their advisors would make them feel bad, saying that taking money from the portfolio was a big mistake. Therefore, I have tried to teach people to change their perceptions of their advisors by comparing them with car salesmen.

When I think of a car salesman, I don't think of a friend; I think of someone whose first job is to sell me a car. I also have a mental image of a guy with a wrinkled shirt and a clip-on tie who is asking me for a credit report before I can close the door of my vehicle. I understand that his job is to sell me a car, and any questions or concerns all revolve around the main goal of selling the vehicle so that he, the salesman, will get a commission check. Whether my notion of a car salesman is right or wrong, I view the experience of buying a new car as similar to that of a financial manager, one seeking to cash *his* commission check using *your* money.

When a person thinks of a money manager, she sees someone who is wise, interesting, and charming and someone who has your best interest at heart. We don't think of money managers as self-driven, but rather driven by the return they can provide for their clients. We think of our money managers as people who want to help others, but in reality, their goal is to earn their check the same way a car salesman earns his, by selling you his service. If you have ever used a money manager, then you may have noticed that a money manager's goals and your goals do not always align. A money manager's goal is to have as many assets under management as possible. If you are someone like my friend Tara, who has excess of $500,000 in assets with a money manager, then chances are your relationship will be good with the advisor. I am not suggesting that money managers are bad people, but I am implying that people allow emotions to get in the way while making decisions about handling their own finances or even whether or not to even shop for another firm to handle their finances. As stated previously, if you are going to trust someone with your money, it would have to be a special kind of person. Think about it, how many people in your life would you trust with all your money? My guess is not many, yet we allow ourselves to give full control to money management firms, who are people we really don't even know.

If you buy a car at a dealership, you are most likely going to pay a higher price because you are letting the professionals sell it to you. Likewise, when you buy a security with a money manager, you are paying a much higher premium than if you bought the security yourself through an online brokerage firm because you are letting the professionals buy the security. The only difference is that anyone can buy a security, but you can't create a car and finance it from thin air. Therefore, the car salesman provides more value. In both professions, the number one goal is to sell as much of the product or service as possible. The goal is to convince prospective clients that they are getting the best deal, brand, or service that cannot be provided anywhere else.

It is your personal obligation to view the person handling your money the same way you would any other business transaction or any other person hired to perform a service. If you are dissatisfied or feel as though you are getting a poor deal, it is merely common sense that you should walk away and not worry about hard feelings. Trust me, if your money were to run out, or if you were to take your business elsewhere, there would be very few small-talk conversations or days on the golf course between you and your current money manager. Once again, it's the same concept as when a car salesman spends hours with you to get the best possible sale. The only difference is that money managers must continue to work with you so that they can keep your business.

Now that we have discussed the thought process of both money managers and clients, let's take a look at the performance of money managers. The key to deciding on whether or not you will handle your own finances should be determined by your level of satisfaction with your portfolio. Therefore, let's look at the areas that your money manager may not discuss with you as a client and allow me to explain why managing finances is the only industry in the world where a loss can be measured as a success.

MEASURE OF SUCCESS (FOR YOUR MONEY MANAGER)

Did you know that the majority of money managers have either performed with or underperformed the S&P 500 over the last 12 years? If you incorporate the number of money managers who barely beat the market, then you are looking at nearly all the money managers throughout the country. Most are either underperforming or barely performing with the S&P 500, and yet they are marketing it as a success.

The fact that money managers mostly perform at or underperform the market does not mean that these people are not superintelligent individuals. There are several reasons that average returns have fallen as of late. First, we endured a recession, and a large number of money managers were invested heavily in the financial sector, which crashed during the housing crisis. Second, the market has traded flat over the last 12 years, which led to more desperate moves to keep unsatisfied clients happy. Lastly, most money managers are goal-oriented by certain benchmarks, which means that a loss can be positive in the eyes of the money manager. This may sound ludicrous to you, but being a successful money manager is sometimes measured by performance against an index, not an overall return. If the manager outperforms the index by only a fraction, it is great for his or her marketing campaign and is measured as a success.

A DIFFERENCE IN GOALS

A money manager's goal is simple: She must get as many assets under management as possible. There is a theory among the general public that fund managers only get paid if you make money. In fact, money managers typically make money on initial and closing fees or get higher percentages based on the total amount managed. A money manager may charge you an annual amount based on the size of your portfolio, or she may charge you a fee for every "buy and sell" of a security. Therefore, she gets paid regardless of performance and benefits from a larger number of assets under management.

What if I told you that the so-called "professionals" underperformed their benchmark on a pre-tax basis by about 1.8 percent per year. Would you still be so optimistic and supportive of your money manager? In *The Quest for Alpha*, Larry Swedroe begins his book by discussing a study performed by Mark Carhart and three colleagues where they analyzed 2,071 equity funds for a period of 33 years and found that the average fund underperformed its "benchmark" by this 1.8 percent margin. To many this won't make sense because these are the professionals who are supposed to be the "wizards" of the market. However, because of large fees and "index chasing" you can be more successful than the high-profile fund managers, although I am certain that you will want bigger returns for you and your family.

The key with this study is the word "benchmark," which is a focus for a particular fund. A fund will typically trade certain stocks in their investment strategy, or fund, such as small caps, large caps, energy or financial stocks. As a result, at the end of the year the firm will compare their performance to the performance of an index, or the industry of companies that is being monitored by their fund. I know it sounds confusing, but this is how much of Wall Street works. The most popular strategy is to track the S&P 500, therefore no matter what, the firm will perform closely with the S&P 500 on a yearly basis, but will always be behind because of large fees. As a result some firms will add other investments to try and close the gap, but based on the study above, it's rare. However, when a firm does outperform their benchmark it is a cause for celebration and is a great marketing tool to grow the fund larger. Because at the end of the day, the goal is to grow the fund larger to collect larger fees and put more money in their pocket.

A money manager who outperforms a benchmark can market herself as having great returns because money managers measure their success against a particular index or class of stocks. So even though the market has lost or traded flat, a money manager can market herself as a wizard who has outperformed the market even if the gain is only 1 percent, which underperforms all other investments. For example, if a money manager was overweight (invested heavily) in financials during the recession or had a large-cap financial fund that outperformed the performance of the S&P 500 financial sector, that firm could correctly advertise themselves as outperforming the sector, even if you and everyone else who invests with the firm lost 15 percent of their worth. This is important, so I'll say it again: It doesn't matter if the index loses 5, 10, 15, or even 20 percent; as long as the firm does a little better (even if it's a loss) than the index, it is a win on Wall Street, and for the firm.

It is important that all investors come to the realization that your goals and a money manager's goals more than likely do not align. I am not saying that money managers don't want great returns or that there aren't any great money managers because there are some who will spend much time doing research and are worth every penny. The majority, however, care only about outperforming the S&P 500, even if the index is trading with a 10 percent loss. As long as the manager loses only 5 percent, she has performed 100 percent better than the market, and that is a very marketable fact to people who don't fully understand the measure of success on Wall Street. As a result, the money manager makes more money by attracting new clients and still takes commission costs from you while sometimes losing your money and calling it a success.

A MORE INTELLIGENT FORM OF INVESTING

Let's say that you have $100,000, and you want a money manager to invest the money. We have already discussed money managers being driven by the performance of various indexes. Therefore, the money manager may purchase a fund that mirrors the S&P 500, which is most commonly referred to as "SPY." Now, if the money manager purchases SPY, he could very well charge you north of $2,000 just to buy the security. If you open up an online brokerage account, it could cost you less than $100 to invest the same amount while diversifying the money yourself.

I remember having a discussion with a previous coworker when I worked as a counselor, and he saying that he used to manage his own money until he lost too much. Now he lets the professionals handle his money. The fact of the matter is that there is minimal research to suggest that "professionals" return better gains than individual investors. As stated previously, the advancements in technology and research make it easier than ever before to take control of your own financial future. Therefore, there is no time like the present to step out of your comfort zone and take control of your own personal investments.

The truth is that no one cares more about your money than you. Since you are the one who worked long hours and often had to make sacrifices while earning your income, no one is going to have the same level of concern, attention, and respect as you. Therefore, the key becomes learning how to take control and knowing where to start in order to return the best possible gains for you investments.

Throughout this book I am going to give you guidelines that cover everything that has allowed me to succeed. The methods and strategies in this book are what I have used myself to arrive at a place in my life where I can invest full time and live stress-free because I am financially secure. This book will discuss all the common mistakes, and you will get a chance to experience some of the mistakes that I currently still make. Hopefully, you will learn from my own mistakes and become a successful investor. Whether you are a person who has never invested or a seasoned veteran looking for new strategies, my goal is to give you the knowledge that will return larger gains, as well as understanding when to buy, when to sell, and how to identify strong companies. So let's get started on the journey of becoming a successful investor and learn how to make money in this new era of trading, regardless of your goals.

CHAPTER 2

Economic Outlook

I never attempt to make money on the stock market.
I buy on the assumption that they could close the market
the next day and not reopen it for five years.

—WARREN BUFFET

THE FIRST STEP

The first step toward building a winning portfolio strategy is not fundamental analysis or looking at charts but rather creating an economic picture for both the present and the future. This important step is so often forgotten but is very important in determining how you will diversify your portfolio. The goal is to look at where the market is headed, based on where it has been, and identify which sectors, industries, or technologies could rise based on current value.

Trying to predict the future trend of the market can be very difficult and even somewhat dangerous because assumptions often can lead to lifelong trouble for investors. I prefer looking back at the past and forming a strategy based on the mind-set of investors and our current economic climate. The old saying, "Hope for the best, but plan for the worst," is entirely relevant in this situation. We want to become realists during this time and not look at the economy as economic indicators that move the market on a daily basis but rather as factors that affect everyday people such as you and me.

The first thing we need to look at is what has influenced investors in the past. The past is important because it affects our present and even distorts our outlook for the future. Since 1999, we have lived through the dot-com bubble and the recession of 2008, which caused the worst financial environment since the Great Depression. As a result, the Standard and Poor's 500 Index (S&P 500), which is perhaps the best source of information on the health of our economy, lost more than 10 percent of its value between January 2000 and 2012. Anyone who invested in the dot-com new technology or in the financial system experienced a devastating blow to their portfolios. As a result, these events have affected the thought process and outlook for a large number of investors.

THE DOT-COM BUBBLE

If ever you become a long-term investor, chances are that you will live through and experience an economic bubble or possibly many such bubbles. These bubbles are industries, a group of stocks, a technology, or anything else that trades and is valued way above its intrinsic value. These are ridiculous valuations for companies that cannot be logically valued. The key to these bubbles is that they become a market sensation but then lose value, affecting other areas of business very abruptly, often as quickly as they develop.

You may be thinking that bubbles such as the dot-com bubble would be easy to identify, but during the time period I am discussing, even prominent companies such as Corning (GLW), Cisco (CSCO), and Global Crossing were caught in the moment. Furthermore, they even changed their business models to support the demand and growth of the bubble. Unfortunately, they were crushed once the demand diminished.

The interesting fact regarding bubbles is that they force everyone to get caught up in the moment, including the largest companies with the smartest managers. The Internet bubble in particular was very speculative in nature, but it was something new and was something that had never been experienced. The Internet presented a business-based structure where supplies and services were more readily and cheaply available, meaning that investors saw opportunity and inappropriately valued companies presenting this structure.

During the Internet bubble, companies with very little revenue and hardly any earnings could become public companies based purely on speculation and ideas alone. Some companies, such as Amazon (AMZN) and Google (GOOG), used this situation, along with low interest rates, as a time to develop and grow, and they have stood the test of time. Others, however, such as Pets.com, may go down in history as some of the worst valuations of all time.

Most dot-com companies have since filed for bankruptcy, or were acquired and sold for much less than their relative worth. Some of the more infamous examples include GeoCities, one of the longer-lived dot-com companies, which was bought by Yahoo (YHOO) for $3.57 billion, before closing 10 years later. Then there was The Learning Company, bought by Mattel for a whopping $3.5 billion and sold one year later for just $27.3 million. These are just a couple of examples, but unfortunately, the list is quite long of acquisitions and valuations that fell into this category and depreciated very quickly.

You may be wondering how a company can devalue at such a rapid rate; that part of the bubble is what I call *the realization*. It occurs when investors and all of what the companies acquired fit into the bubble and then wonder, What the hell was I thinking? It is first sparked by an event that makes those who invest react to the valuation. During the dot-com bubble, the technology-heavy Nasdaq Index went from an all-time high of 5,132.52 to below 1,200.00 in just two years. All Internet-based companies were affected; Amazon crashed to $16 a share, and Cisco, one of the companies that invested heavily in the Internet bubble's success, lost 86 percent of its value, whereas Corning went from over $110 to just $2 a share in two years.

The excitement and ultimate sorrow that were experienced during this time taught us that Internet companies can be successful but not indispensable. The early years after the turn of the century were perhaps the most overly optimistic period of the last 20 years, but excessive optimism eventually creates a crash, which is exactly what happened. Sarah Lacy explains in her book, *Once You're Lucky, Twice You're Good*, the powerful presence of optimism that took control of our logic during the dot-com era. She talks about how market experts were constantly featured in magazines and such, explaining the reasons that a tech resurrection was "just a quarter or two away." Meanwhile, the Nasdaq continued to fall, and many investors lost much of their wealth as a result of the bubble, which clouded their judgment and logic.

As an investor, you can learn from experiences such as these by trying to identify the possible bubbles that appear to look favorable; to ride higher, but you also must learn to know when to get out. Also, you must learn to identify the behaviors that caused us to throw logic out the window and invest in overvalued entities that could barely be classified as companies.

Now, in this second decade of the new millennium, we are seeing a new breed of Internet companies based on the concept of communication and social media. The Internet bubble evolved because it was all about providing a service or a product through the Internet, but now we are seeing companies such as Facebook, LinkedIn, and Twitter, all returning revenue from advertising, that still have gaudy valuations. This craze has even moved into other countries, with companies such as Renren, Rediff, and Yandex. Therefore, we have to ask ourselves if this is the start of yet another Internet bubble, or have we finally got it right? Will this iteration of the Internet company be a prosperous investment? Regarding this decision and/or outlook, I'd like to refer to an old proverb, "Fool me once, shame on you; fool me twice, shame on me," meaning that a person shouldn't allow himself or herself to be fooled by lies, bad deals, or any other forms of trickery.

THE RECESSION—THAT CUT US DEEP

The recession of 2008–2009 was an event that will have long-lasting effects that far outweigh our current knowledge. This event was a result of us getting too comfortable in the economy, financing homes, cars, and other luxuries that we simply could not afford. It may have been the result of an irresponsible banking industry, but it also was an accumulated deficit caused by the administration, consumers, and our inability to act in a reasonable manner.

Because the recession is only a few years old, most people remember clearly the details and how they affected individual people and their families. In a matter of months, individuals lost nearly 30 percent of their retirement investments, such as 401(k) plans. Housing prices also plummeted, reflecting large losses in what was most people's largest investment. In addition, corporate earnings fell, and unemployment skyrocketed, providing further complement to Americans losing the security of their investments. For many Americans, the economic downturn is still very much alive. Many will now have to work longer hours while enjoying fewer luxuries as they try to erase that place in time that is considered by some to be the worst economic period in the history of the United States.

There have been books, movies, and countless hours of media coverage discussing the recession of 2008–2009. Therefore, it would be nearly impossible to cover all the issues and the domino effect, which ultimately created an economic environment that affected so many people and institutions. One of my favorite movies (and books) is *Too Big to Fail*, by Andrew Ross Sorkin. It is one of the few times that I actually enjoyed the movie more than the book, even though the book was very well written. The movie allows you to see and feel the panic of Wall Street's leaders, providing a better understanding of the sequence of events that occurred and how each occurred. I urge everyone to take time and study the recession. Study the dot-com bubble and all other periods of economic distress, and increase your knowledge and awareness of their effects.

GETTING BURNED HAS ITS EFFECTS

The recession of 2008–2009 created the worst financial environment since the Great Depression, which nearly collapsed the entire financial system. The dot-com bubble was a period that nearly collapsed a number of powerhouse companies and led to many bad decisions on behalf of both investors and established corporations, along with affecting portfolio returns. You may wonder what these two events have in common in terms of Wall Street, besides creating a flat market. Another concern is how they will affect our future, considering the irreversible damage that has already been done.

One trend that we can identify is that these recessions and harsh economic environments are getting more and more difficult to fix. We are not an economy that relies on only the United States for prosperity, but we also rely on emerging markets and global trade to maintain our quality of life. Therefore, when trade is disrupted or local economies suffer, it directly affects other economies, spreading like cancer. The minute one problem is fixed, another one can arise, sometimes one that is even more complex than the original problem. This keeps the global economy from reaching a point where it is completely sufficient and also affects the outlook and actions of both consumers and corporations.

Perhaps the most difficult situation following the recession has been the unemployment rate. The high unemployment rate is a result of corporations either not hiring or laying off workers. But what has consumers and protesters, such as Occupy Wall Street, so angry is that several of the largest corporations are posting their all-time highest earnings. Obviously, this is something that would create a great deal of frustration, so let's look at why corporations aren't hiring, which will serve as your first lesson into the psyche of Wall Street.

I want you to take a moment to think back to when you were a child and you touched something hot. Chances are that it was a stove, toaster, or maybe a curling iron—no matter what it may have been, the end result was that it inflicted pain. Most likely you did not like the feeling of getting burned; therefore, the burn was a negative reinforcement that kept you from continuing to touch the hot object. Such feelings are created in our brain and allow us to learn from our mistakes. In other words, our brain sends a message of pain when we do something that causes us discomfort to make sure that it does not happen again. On the contrary, we are provided positive reinforcement for actions such as eating, an action that is necessary for stopping hunger pangs.

What people don't realize is that the dot-com bubble and the financial crisis both caused negative reinforcement, which was the result of companies investing too much into the Internet boom's success, having too many employees during economic struggles, and operating with too much financing, along with a fair share of bad decisions. These situations, among others, are now affecting the way that large corporations are conducting business, which is increased efficiency without unnecessary expenses. So far there has been little incentive for these companies to hire in a way that will have an impact on the economy; therefore, they do not, and although helping themselves, they are hurting the economy.

Over the past 10 years, even the most financially secure companies have faced harsh challenges and have since had to evolve. As a result, companies are attempting to maximize profits in order to have more cash. In this way, in the event of another economic catastrophe, they will be better prepared. We must face the fact that some companies probably can't handle another catastrophe. Therefore, all are hoping for the best but preparing for the worst—and honestly, I don't blame them. Most people, after getting burned once, will change their behavior. Corporate America got burned twice; therefore, companies are taking extra precautions to ensure that it won't happen again.

The unemployment picture in America and the mind-set of corporate America related to employment is just one of many dominos that all come together to affect our economy. You also must consider the rising costs of goods and the price of gasoline while consumer income stays the same. In some ways, therefore, you can say that large corporations are increasing their margins at the expense of yours.

The point of the "getting burned" analogy explains one of the many reasons why a corporation earning billions may not hire people who make $50,000 annually. It doesn't necessarily make sense, but it does give us some insight into how the corporations that make up the market view the economy. It also helps to provide us with a mental vision of how they will operate over the next 10 years. Unless given a reason to hire or some sort of incentive, we can expect corporations to ensure that they do not get burned in the future because the next burn could be a wild fire.

WHAT HAPPENS NEXT?

The future trend of the market is the most highly debated subject in our financial media, each broadcast being inconsistent with others. For example, you probably could turn your channel to Fox, CNN, or CNBC right now and watch for 20 minutes and hear at least four different opinions, from four very intelligent people, that differ on the direction of the market. You will find this on all business or economic broadcasts. The future is unwritten and unknown by any human on earth, and we don't have the ability to speak in absolutes. We can voice our opinions, but no one knows for sure what will happen over the next decade.

My theory, the best way to invest, is to prepare for a flat market; the only way to prepare for a flat market is to invest in value. It is obvious that the mind-set on Wall Street is rapidly changing and has been affected over the last 10 years. These bear markets are getting more complex over time because there are simply too many moving parts. It is very possible that we will see a bull market in the next 10 years because corporate earnings are so strong. The economy should see improvements in the housing industry, along with other areas that I will discuss. However, it is very possible that we could enter into another recession owing to the struggles in Europe or a bubble that has yet been identified. This is what's so devastating about a bubble—you never see it coming.

HOW SHOULD I INVEST IN THE MARKET?

If you ask 10 different analysts or any other brilliant minds in the market industry, you probably would get several different views concerning market performance in the next decade. We simply don't know. We can make predictions based on what we currently know, but we cannot be sure of how the market will perform or what events will affect the market over the next 10 years.

On Wall Street, there are thousands of brilliant people with many years of education from the best financial programs in this country. Yet not one pair shares the exact same portfolio (unless, of course, they share the same firm). There are more publically traded companies than people in my home town in Tennessee, and each company has an institutional investor among thousands and sometimes millions of individual investors who believe in the company and its future. Therefore, if there was a one-stop-shop for perfection and guaranteed results, then all investors would just buy a handful of companies, and everyone would get rich. Unfortunately, for every buyer, there is a seller, and you can't make money unless someone else is losing money or willing to buy shares at a higher price than you paid for your shares.

The bottom line is that our market has no logical, methodical trading habits. We can look at a chart and find comparisons if we look hard enough, but it is constantly evolving with the growth or demise of the economy and with each and every day being truly unique. Therefore, the only way to ensure success is to follow an old Warren Buffett quote: "If a business does well, its stock usually follows." Then, once you find this company, find an attractive price that offers value.

I will explain in detail throughout this book that sometimes the market behaves in a way that cannot be explained logically, and stocks that should trade higher will trade lower. Contrarily, there are also stocks that should trade lower yet will trade higher, and the valuations simply will not make sense when compared with similar companies. My goal is to teach you how to identify these discrepancies and profit from a market that could very well trade flat over the next 10 years. The only way that I know how to profit from these inconsistencies is to invest in value, which means to identify *why* a stock is trading lower. Then you capitalize, when it's nothing more than a domino effect of fear and panic.

CHAPTER 3

Myth Versus Reality

Don't Make Assumptions. Find the courage to ask
questions and to express what you really want.
Communicate with others as clearly as you can to avoid
misunderstandings, sadness and drama. With just this
one agreement, you can completely transform your life.

—MIGUEL ANGEL RUIZ

Before we get started and dig into the fundamentals of a company
and the psyche of investors, it is important to discuss a few of the
basic assumptions and risks of investing. If you are new to investing
and have never considered taking control of your own portfolio until
now, then first off, congratulations, but second, you probably have
a long list of concerns regarding this decision. Earlier I called this
decision an overly emotional period in a person's life. The reason
that it is overly emotional is that we psych ourselves out in preparation and are sometimes scared before we even start because of what
we have been taught to believe about investing.

To this day, one of my biggest shortcomings is my desire to
predict or make assumptions about the market. This can be due to

one of two things: either overconfidence or a lack of confidence. In a later chapter I will talk in detail about assumptions and behavioral characteristics that cause problems, but for now, you should know that these assumptions are what usually cause trouble for investors. Because we are human, though, assumptions are a part of our personality, therefore making them nearly impossible to consistently avoid. Before we get started, let's take some time to discuss some of the most common misconceptions about investing so that you can continue with a clear train of thought and open yourself to the notion that you can be successful in this "new era" of trading, even if others tell you that you cannot.

FIVE ASSUMPTIONS TO INVESTING

One of the most significant reasons we make investment mistakes is because we set unrealistic goals, seek complexity, and make assumptions that simply aren't true. In 2007, my attitude toward investing began to change. I had always shown an interest in behavioral finance, but in 2007 I considered myself successful and felt comfortable enough to begin giving advice and talking to other investors and prospective investors. The first thing I noticed when talking to both new investors and people who wanted to manage their own portfolios is that there are several assumptions that underlie investing. I noticed that people really look up to others who work in the financial field and believe that market success is a magic trick of some sort.

I've identified five key assumptions to investing that almost all prospective investors believe. If you are a new investor, then you may believe one of these assumptions, but separating from the belief is one of the first steps in becoming a logical thinking, successful value investor.

1. People Who Invest Are Rich

Before I began investing, I believed that active investors had to be considerably wealthy. This belief was the result of several factors, including how I was treated when I spoke to financial advisors and even the people I knew who were active investors. When I first began investing, I had less than $10,000, which is a fact that people are very surprised to hear when they speak with me. The truth is that I started small, made good investments, made several sacrifices to my lifestyle, and continued to work hard and add money to my portfolio over a period of many years.

Almost everyone who has achieved wealth had to start small. Whether they started with a small business and grew it into a multi-billion-dollar corporation or had a good idea and capitalized on that idea, they started off at the bottom and had to work their way to the top. Obviously, this excludes "trust-fund babies" and people who hit the lottery, but anyone with a genuine talent or a level of skill had to work for their wealth. Unfortunately, a major misconception of investing is that the majority of investors are wealthy. According to Fidelity, the average 401(k) balance was $71,500 at the end of 2010, which was a 10-year high. This average is compiled from a participant base of 11 million accounts. And although there are many factors involved, such as age, profession, employment length, and so on, this still puts an end to the assumption that all investors are wealthy. In fact, most are everyday people who make up the "99 percent." This belief that you must be wealthy to be an investor is simply not true, with the average portfolio, according to Fidelity, being less than $75,000, and this is, of course, dependent on age and years in the workforce.

The misconception and belief that all active investors are wealthy actually hinders some people from learning and asking questions. Our society is very intimidated by those who have wealth. It forces us to be jealous and make bad decisions, but more important, a lack of wealth causes us to feel inferior. Unfortunately, our society does not judge people on their personality, kindness, or loyalty, but rather associates a person with their worldly possessions.

Most people would rather not ask questions than take the chance of feeling embarrassed. I remember when I was 18 years old. I had a balance in my bank account of $3.51. I knew I had a charge that was going to cause my account to be negative, but I couldn't force myself to deposit enough money to cover the charge. I needed to deposit $7 to cover the charge, but I only had $20 in cash and didn't get paid for two more days. I had investments but wasn't able to access the money in the time that I needed. Therefore, I was faced with a dilemma: I could either deposit the $7 to avoid an overcharge, or I could limit the embarrassment and take my chances. Like a moron, I took my chances and was too embarrassed to approach the teller with a deposit slip for $7.

My story may be funny to look back on, but it's a good example of the choices and feelings that a lack of financial security can cause in a person's life. I ended up with a $30 overdraft fee because I did not want to approach a teller with a $7 deposit slip. The truth is that most tellers have seen it all. Most likely I could have deposited $3, and the teller would have had a lower deposit at some point during his or her career. This fear is a reality for most people, and it causes us to make stupid decisions when faced with a situation where someone else knows our financial status.

The assumption that all active investors are wealthy has several psychological effects that potential investors must overcome before they can better themselves. The idea that someone else may know your financial status is scary to some people, and for some, who are forced to seek help on occasion, it's demoralizing. But you shouldn't let fear of rejection affect your willingness to learn and act in a way that could benefit your financial future. There are a number of intelligent individuals in the financial industry who can help to educate you on building a better financial future, but you must be willing to talk and open up your deepest secret, which is your financial status. You may get some who turn you down or treat you badly, but I guarantee that such a stance will help you in the long run. You can start investing with whatever you want, and it doesn't have to be a million dollars. The truth is that very few people have a million dollars, and most started off small, even in the prideful world of investing. It is nothing more than a misconception that all active investors are rich. Most are just like you and have had the same fears and misgivings, but they acted on the fears and are now bettering themselves, regardless of what some teller thinks.

2. Investing Is Too Complex

The assumption that investing is too complex could be made a reality very easily. The good thing about investing is that it can be as easy or as difficult as you please. There are some people who want to appear most intelligent, and they choose to use complex systems for selecting investments. The people who choose to find a needle in a haystack are defensive and irrational toward those who simply go and get a new needle. Both require work, but the end result is the same—both parties get their needle.

This complexity assumption includes the belief that the more research you perform, the better return you will get on your investment. My belief is that you need due diligence, you need to know your goals, and you need to understand fundamental research, but you also need to know what's most important to the market. If you research for three weeks and arrive at a conclusion and I research for three hours and determine that I am going to purchase the same stock, does the difference really matter? The idea that research is not required is ignorant. However, I am living proof that you can build your own system based on value investing and behavioral finance and make a significant amount of money in this market. There are hundreds of fast-growing companies that are traded on one of the large exchanges. But the level of return is going to be determined by when you purchase a particular stock, which I believe is the most important area of research and is determined simply by understanding the behavior of the market.

The phrase, "Pick and choose your battles," is very important in the field of investing. This relates to every aspect of investing: how you feel about a particular company, when to buy, research, fundamentals, technicals, and so on. People have all sorts of different preferences when it comes to the best way to invest. Some focus more on the fundamentals, which means to base an investment decision on the growth of the company, its industry's growth, and other pieces of measurable data. Then there are others who focus mostly on technical indicators, which means they base investing decisions on charts. These people watch for certain trends to occur. They pay attention to the many indicators that tell them when a stock is oversold, or they may watch for changes in volume. I believe the best choice by far is to invest purely on fundamentals, but then incorporate the behavior and value of the market to find the perfect entry point.

There are over 1,700 publically traded companies that have more than 500,000 shares traded per day. Obviously, I don't believe that each of these stocks would make good investments, but obviously, some would disagree. Remember, investing is very emotional, and every company has a number of investors who buy its stock. Therefore, this proves that all research is different, and there are numerous ways for an investor to arrive at different conclusions. I don't think there is one standard way to invest, but I chose a form of value investing that involves limiting emotion, finding companies with solid fundamentals, and then entering at a cheap price. As a result, I do not believe that complex systems are needed to be a successful investor, but I also believe that complex systems are common and are used as a way of showing one's knowledge.

3. I Can't Do it Myself

One of the hardest assumptions to overcome is the feeling of inadequacy or the idea that you are incapable of becoming a personal investor. Regardless of the strategy employed, some people become so heavily reliant on their brokers that they can't mentally break free. The reasons for not taking control are limitless, but one of the more common ones that I hear has to do with the broker-client relationship.

An investor can have a genuinely strong relationship with the person who handles his money. It makes sense. If money is one of the more important aspects of your life and you are trusting it to a particular person, then you better have a good relationship. The relationship is positive unless it begins to cloud your judgment, such as with my friend Tara.

Most excuses that people provide to defend their lack of action relates to a loyalty of some sort to their financial advisor or broker. But you only live once, and when you are dealing with your hard-earned retirement money, it's too important to let emotional attachments be involved. You must make the decisions that are best for you and your family, even though, of course, your advisor wants you to stay. He is probably pocketing 4 percent of every transaction on your behalf. The bottom line is that you can do it yourself, and it will cost much less—and the rewards most likely will be greater.

4. I Must Take Risks to Be Successful

I am often told that the buy-and-hold strategy is dead and that investors are no longer satisfied with a 15 percent return. First, I disagree with the buy-and-hold strategy being dead, but I agree that investors are no longer satisfied with minimum returns. Thanks to technology, our society wants instant results and shows a genuine lack of patience. This lack of patience is often seen in equity markets as the perfect combination of volatility, money, and emotion that creates the most illogical reactions known to humankind. As a result, people labor under the assumption that the markets are too risky and that the only way to make money in the markets is to take a large number of risks.

The idea that you must take significant risks to succeed is highly inaccurate. With every investment comes a level of risk. No matter what you buy, there is risk. In equity markets, the significant risk exists for swing and day traders, but not necessarily for people who have long-term goals or can afford and are willing to endure some bad days for a large return. Investors who day trade or have only short-term goals in mind usually end up achieving a much smaller return than those who hold for an extended amount of time.

I have never considered myself a short- or long-term investor but rather an opportunist. I won't sell until the price I set is reached, unless something unexpected occurs that changes the business of the company. I don't panic or react to the market's day-to-day movement, which is the opposite of short-term traders, who panic the first day their stock trades lower. Then, because of commission costs and too many days of loss, these investors almost always return a much smaller gain.

It's the most uneasy feeling in the world to watch $3,000 disappear. But if you invest, the chances are that there will come a day when a stock you own will either fall by a large margin or you will wait and take profits too late and lose out on a potentially larger return. However, such days are limited, and by using the tools in this book successfully, you can buy good companies low and sell high while limiting risk, which is the ultimate goal of investing.

5. I Don't Have the Time

I hate the excuse of not having time to become a self-sufficient investor because I don't understand what is more important than your future. The level of involvement that you allow for your portfolio doesn't necessarily determine the level of your gains per year. However, successful investing does require time—but not as much as you may think.

Throughout the remainder of this book I will discuss a number of strategies and ways to buy and sell stocks that require minimal involvement but return the maximum level of reward. In fact, some may argue that investors who are too active actually perform worse because they have trouble taking profit as a result of always wanting more and are quick to react when faced with the fear of loss. I do feel that being a value investor will provide you with the maximum level of gains because of the characteristics that I describe, which include staying calm.

RISK OF INVESTING

The most obvious risk of investing is that you will lose all your money. This idea of risk is a misconception. Obviously, there is a level of risk for any investor, but that level is nowhere near what the general public believes, people who insist that money managers and Wall Street types control all the wealth and take it from the little people. I can't count how many times someone has said to me that she doesn't understand why I invest because it's too risky. The truth is quite the contrary because risk and investing do go hand in hand, but what's great about investing is that you can limit your risk by having realistic expectations.

If your goal is to return 300 percent per year for 10 years, then chances are that you're taking some massive risks. The first thing to consider and understand is that investing is not gambling. You are not playing blackjack, betting on horses, or playing the slot machines and praying that it hits a triple jackpot. Rather, you are owning a piece of a company that you believe will grow.

There are many different ways to invest, and if your goal is to limit the risk, then chances are that you will want to invest for value and in companies that return capital to their investors in dividends. In my opinion, risk assessment is something that must be decided on by individual investors along with their families. If you are a 50-year-old man who is nearing retirement, then you probably don't want to take too many risks on companies that aren't yet established.

One of the best ways to protect yourself from loss is to have a portfolio that consists of a variety of investments. As we get older, our willingness to take risk should diminish, and our concentration should turn to maintenance while still returning a gain that is better than the norm.

In today's volatile market, some people are weary of investing in equities. There have been a large number of events over the last 15 years to create pessimism in equity markets. We've had a housing crisis that destroyed the value of large banks, along with a dot-com bubble burst that also resulted in a massive hit to the market. These two examples are not reasons to avoid U.S. equity markets but rather be smarter and more realistic and realize that we are in a new era. Success in the market can be achieved, but it's a different game than it was in the 1980s and 1990s, an era that I call the bull era.

The bull era was a period in time where the economy was booming, consumers were buying, and the markets were trading higher. During a period of 20 years, from 1980 to 2000, the Dow Jones Industrial Average rose from around 850 to greater than 11,500. The terms *bull* and *bear* refer to the direction and outlook of the market. When it's trading higher with a positive outlook, we refer to it as a *bull market*. But when the market is trading lower and there are rising concerns, we refer to it as a *bear market*. Obviously, because of the market's large returns prior to the year 2000, we can say with certainty that it was indeed a bull market. Yet, because of the bull era and the market's flat performance over the last 13 years, some have left equity markets for investments they consider to be safer and less volatile.

A popular choice for individuals nearing retirement is to invest their hard-earned money in saving accounts or bonds. I have no problem with investors deciding to invest a portion of their savings in these two investments, but I believe that the reason these choices are so popular among near retirees is that such people are unaware of the safer options and larger rewards that are available in equity markets.

Ultimately, it is the decision of you and your families as to how to invest your money. I believe that at this moment, because of fear and recent economic events, U.S. equity markets present the greatest value compared with commodities, global exchanges, or any bonds. People simply don't realize the value within the market, which is why I am going to spend the rest of this book looking at, defining, and finding value, and the reasons for that value, in the market.

CHAPTER 4

Value Investing ...
Or Something Like It

Whether we're talking about socks or stocks, I like buying
quality merchandise when it is marked down.

—WARREN BUFFETT

Take a minute to research the documentation that is available to
explain value investing as a paradigm. Try Google, and read through
any of the 16.4 million search results that will be found when you
type "value investing." Or better yet, read an annual report from
Warren Buffett or any of the many revisions to Benjamin Graham's
book, *The Intelligent Investor*, and you will find a comprehensive
guideline for the practice of value investing.

The bottom line is that there is a huge amount of information
out there regarding value investing as a practice, so much that if you
are interested in pursuing the strategy, then it won't be difficult.
What will be difficult is sticking with the strategy once you adopt
it, seeing as how many know the moves of value investing but fail to
practice them.

When I first began writing this book, my biggest concern was finding a way to define *value investing* that would be both easy to understand and simple to practice. While trying to decide on how to present value investing, I thought of my uncle Greg.

Greg is a very intelligent man who lives in a small town, where he's been the principal at the local elementary school for decades. I live near Cincinnati, which is a 3½-hour drive for Greg. Once a month, though, Greg will drive to Cincinnati on a Friday and will leave on Sunday. He comes up here once a month for a hobby, or job, that he loves—"yard saling."

Greg will stake out all the local yard sales and plan his attack. He will sometimes go to seven different places on any given Saturday, and he even coordinates his attack based on locations that will be open first and that are in the best neighborhoods. Then, on Saturday morning, Greg wakes up before dawn and sorts through other people's junk in search for a "diamond in the ruff." The amount of money that he will spend is limitless but his goal is to buy things that other people will use and then sell them at the flea market on Sunday morning.

I remember one time in particular when Greg had been out all morning and came back with two carfuls of "stuff." He told me that he'd only spent $120, yet he had bought tools, picture frames, furniture, tables, and so on. He then went to the flea market, paid his $30 fee to set up shop, and waited for potential buyers. To make a long story short, Greg stayed at the flea market for five hours and came back with over $500—and still had half his initial "stuff." Therefore, his return on his investment made the research and work worth the time, and given that he returned with valuable "stuff" left over, he still had the ability to return more gains at a later time.

Some of you may be wondering how my uncle's hobby relates to value investing. The fact is that in all reality, Greg was acting as a value investor and didn't even realize it.

To be a good value investor, you need all the same traits that my uncle Greg uses to be successful at returning a profit from yard saling. You need to do research, you have to seek value through what some may consider junk, then you need to purchase at a value price, and finally, you need to have patience and wait for a sizable return.

Just as Greg spent time researching his "attack" on yard sales, you have to invest in research to become a successful investor. You need to read books, know how to understand an earnings report, and identify growth, fundamentals, and stock metrics of a company. I will discuss in great detail the various research materials that you need for success, but for now, it's important that you understand that research is a vital component to success.

The most important factor in determining whether or not a value investor succeeds is the price paid to purchase a stock, similar to how Greg would seek and purchase items at yard sales. When Greg would find an item that he thought could return a profit, he would buy it. A value investor does the same thing: After you've researched and found a large number of potential investments, it's time to narrow them down to investments presenting the most upside. This topic is very broad and complex and will be discussed in greater detail in Chapter 15.

Finally, after Greg buys an item, he prices it much higher, waits, and returns a profit. Unfortunately, we don't have the luxury of buying a stock and then selling it for whatever price we want. Instead, we have to be patient and wait for the stock to appreciate. Here lies the retail investor's biggest problem. The solution, though, is quite simple, as Warren Buffett points out: "Much success can be attributed to inactivity. Most investors cannot resist the temptation to constantly buy and sell." This would be like Greg buying at a yard sale and then immediately selling to the person next to him at the same price. Such a buy is meaningless, but this is a situation that investors often experience.

Value investing can be made very difficult, but when it really comes down to it, all we're doing is buying something cheap and waiting to sell it for more, much like Greg. The only difference is that when Greg buys a table and resells it, it's the same product. An investment appreciates through fundamentals, market conditions, and a company's growth potential. The patience aspect of value investing is by far the most difficult. Most investors have one of two problems: They either don't take profits when they present themselves, or they aren't patient enough to wait for a profit. It's very difficult to find the perfect balance, which is why understanding behavioral finance (Part IV) and your personal shortcomings is so important.

There are a number of different opinions surrounding the true definition of value investing. Some strategies of value investing present a picture that is very difficult and requires genius-level math skills. But others require the ability to think logically and remain calm in the most uneasy of situations. I have built wealth and success simply by performing adequate research, searching for and finding the best stocks that meet my personal goals, investing in those securities, being patient, and waiting for the securities to appreciate. My definition of value investing may differ from that of others, but the bottom line is that value investors are simply searching for stocks that present the most amount of upside compared with cost. You can make it as easy or difficult as you please.

PART II

CHAPTER 5

Income Statement and Quarterly Progress

To make money, buy some good stock, hold it until it
goes up, and then sell it. If it doesn't go up, don't buy it.

—WILL ROGERS

FUNDAMENTALS

I have discussed a wide range of topics, and my goal is that you
should fully understand the purpose of value investing and how it
can be used. You also should keep in mind that regardless of your
goals, you can invest your own money without the use of a money
manager. Now that you understand value investing as a strategy, it's
time to dig into the most important area of becoming a successful
long-term value investor—fundamentals.

The fundamentals of a company are what drive the long-term
direction of a stock. Exercising the practice of research and identifying all data relevant to a company are the essence of fundamental
analysis. Fundamental analysis often can be very tricky and over-

whelming because there are so many areas of research for a particular company. In fact, you could spend hours researching all the data associated with a company's day-to-day operations. Nearly all investment strategies use some form of fundamental analysis. Over the next several chapters I am going to take you inside the fundamentals of a company to help you identify the most important areas so that you will not become overwhelmed with the data.

Investors break fundamental analysis into three areas: *income statement*, *balance sheet*, and *cash flow*. The income statement is perhaps the most often used among investors because it reflects both quarterly and yearly financial data of a company. The balance sheet summarizes a company's cash, total assets, equity, and liabilities for a specific period of time and in my opinion should be the first area of research into a company's performance. The statement of cash flow shows the amount of money that is generated and used by the company. As I discuss these three statements, I will go over terminology to help limit any confusion. Although there are numerous pieces of data, I will not go through every piece, but I will better explain the data that is most beneficial in my analysis and has led to my own success.

INCOME STATEMENT

A company's income statement is the best and easiest way to judge that company's operational progress over a period of time. This piece of data is the single largest market mover for a particular stock. Every quarter, a number of analysts will predict a company's top- and bottom-line results, which means revenue and profit. Both pieces of data are part of the income statement. When a company exceeds expectations, it most likely trades higher, but when a company falls short of expectations, then theoretically the stock will fall lower because it is supposed to be priced according to earnings guidance. Most of the time, though, when you hear people discussing fundamental data, they are discussing information from an income statement. Although there are several events that ultimately can affect the price of a stock, a company's income statement usually reflects stock performance.

In an early chapter I discussed expectations and explained that the market moves up and down as one's expectations rise or fall. When market data, such as a real gross domestic product or employment, are stronger than what we expect, the market moves higher. But when data are below our expectations, the market moves lower until the actual data exceed expectations. The same event occurs with an individual company. We set expectations, and when expectations are exceeded, the stock trades higher. This fact is why it's so important to fully understand fundamentals, along with market psychology (which I will discuss later).

INCOME STATEMENT DATA

Let's take a look at basic fundamental data from an income statement, and I will explain how I use the data as a value investor.

Revenue

Revenue is the amount of money that a company receives during a specific period of time as a result of business activities. This measure on an income statement is one of the most important pieces of data to investors and is referred to as the *top-line number.* When a company announces earnings or the media talks about top-line growth, they are referring to the level at which the company grows revenue over a period of time. This number is important to me as a value investor because it symbolizes growth within the company. My theory is that a company can always figure out a way to cut costs or manipulate taxes, but creating revenue is much more difficult. Therefore, I prefer a company with a large amount of revenue compared with its valuation.

Costs

The *costs* of a company are measured in many areas, but rather than take you inside each of these categories, I will explain costs as one category. As a person, you are fully aware of the definition of *costs*, but in accounting and business, costs are divided into several sections on an income statement. For example, there is a section for selling, general and administrative expenses (SG&A), which are the operational expenses of the company, and they reflect the efficiency of management. Some analysts like to use this particular category of costs as a percentage of total sales to better understand management's efficiency and then track the percentage over a period of time. In addition, a company's cost of goods sold (COGS) is measured to better understand the costs associated with the production of a company's goods. Finally, I personally like to associate special items with a company's costs. A company's special items, which are sometimes referred to as *extraordinary expenses* or *nonrecurring items*, are supposed to be one-time expenses that may affect earnings for a particular quarter. These one-time costs are very important because they can distort the value of a company. Therefore, when looking at the fundamentals, I suggest identifying any large special items. Don't think of them as a negative reflection on the company but rather as a necessary charge that won't affect the company in the following year. In the end, costs are a measure that must be identified and a trend that must be carefully observed. Later I will discuss margins that take into account costs, which I feel is a better way to identify trends and the attractiveness of an investment.

Net Income

My favorite measure for growth is revenue, but the markets prefer net income. *Net income* is the amount of money that a company has, minus expenses, or revenue, minus expenses. It shows how profitable a company is during a specific period of time. Owning a company with a large amount of net income is important because net income ultimately means a stronger balance sheet, which could mean further growth. If a company is not profitable, it obviously will not post net income but will post *net loss* in its place. This is the amount the company lost, after costs from revenue. Net income is very important to the valuation of a company, but as a value investor, I would prefer a profitable company with a greater amount of revenue. A company can easily close offices and lay off employees to return more income, but sooner or later it will reflect as a loss of revenue unless the operations remain consistent.

Pretax Income

A company's *pretax income* is similar to net income, but it's the amount of income prior to taxes. I pay close attention to this particular measure because of the extent to which taxes can be manipulated by a publically traded company.

Earnings per Share

The *earnings per share* (EPS) of a company are perhaps the most important measure to determine the price of a stock. It also goes hand in hand with several important stock metrics. The number most likely reflects the net income of a particular company, but it also takes into account dividends, equity, and the total number of shares. Therefore, the EPS of a $10 billion company may be the same as that of a $1 billion company because the numbers of shares outstanding are different. There is also a possible difference in dividends. As a result, you can't compare the EPS of two different companies, but you can compare a company's EPS performance over a period of several years. This is a very important metric to all investors and is sometimes referred to as the company's *bottom line*.

Profit Margin

A company's *profit margin* isn't something you will necessarily see on that company's income statement, but it can be easily calculated and is very important. The profit margin is how much of every dollar is profit from the company's revenue. It's the net income divided by revenue. This percentage gives you valuable information about the effectiveness of management and the future performance of the company.

For example, let's say a company posts quarterly revenue of $1 billion and a net income of $200 million. Its profit margin would be 20 percent. Now let's say that the company posts revenue of $1.5 billion the following year, during the same quarter, with $255 million in net income. At first glance, the company looks good, with revenue and earnings both increasing, and with this level of growth, the stock may increase. However, the profit margin declined to 17 percent, which means that costs are growing faster than sales. The important thing to remember is that this number is not significant unless it occurs for several quarters or several years in a row. Sometimes a company has to spend money to make money, and if the company endures one quarter of decreased margins to have several quarters of increased margins, then it could be a great investment. You just have to make sure that profit margins are either sustained or improving because they measure the costs of a company.

Operating Margin

The *operating margin* of a company can be measured on a quarterly or yearly basis and is similar to the profit margin. It's used most often as a way to determine how much a company makes per dollar before taxes or interest. Much as with profit margin, the goal of watching this fundamental indicator is to compare its performance over a period of time. I don't typically look at a company's operating margin over a period of quarters, but I do keep track of operating margins over a period of several years. The goal is to make sure that over time this margin is rising with revenue, and the company is becoming more profitable.

Another great way for an investor to use operating margins is to compare two or more companies in similar industries. You may be considering two fast-growing companies in the same industry as a potential investment. When you compare the margins for each company, you may find that one's margins are growing faster than the other's or that one's margins are actually declining. Using both operating and profit margins is a good way to determine the costs for a company, as well as its effectiveness. I don't necessarily care how high the margins are for either profit or operations, but I do care whether or not they are positive and that over a period of several years they are improving, not declining.

USING AN INCOME STATEMENT (TO MAKE A BETTER INVESTMENT)

I am one of the biggest endorsers of Google Finance. The most popular investment research site is probably Yahoo! Finance, but I prefer to use Google Finance on a daily basis when comparing the fundamentals of a company. Since I am a big endorser of Google products, I am going to use the information obtained from Google's income statement to show you how to make an educated investment decision based on the information that I have discussed.

Before I put all the information together, you may notice that there are some areas of the income statement that I failed to mention. My goal, as a value investor and someone teaching you how to improve your returns significantly, is to simplify investing. I talked about complexity, and I am not trying to convince you that I am smarter than you or know the most complex systems for success, but I do want to give you the most effective and simplest road to success that will improve your returns without the complex schemes of any broker. I am yet to discuss several key areas involved in making an investment decision, so I don't want you to worry or get overwhelmed with the countless ways of analyzing a company's income statement. The areas just discussed tell you everything that you need to know about a company's income statement. One piece of information gives you knowledge regarding all other areas of a company's day-to-day operations. With that being said, let's dig deeper and put it all together in order to help you make an educated investing decision based on the income statement alone without worrying about any other aspect of investing.

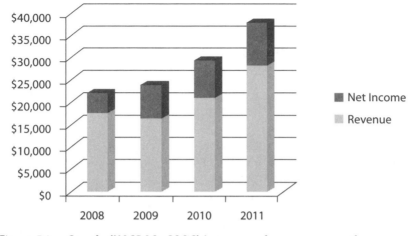

Figure 5.1   **Google (NASDAQ: GOOG) income and revenue growth.**

Figure 5.1 illustrates the amount of revenue and net income over a four-year period for the company Google. As you can see, the company has returned more revenue year over year along with significant jumps in net income. Identifying both revenue and net income should be the first piece of fundamental research that goes into any investment. You may find a company that is growing in both revenue and net income but later find another reason why it may or may not be a good buy. However, if you know that a company is growing, that's your first sign that it could be a candidate for an investment.

After you have identified that a company's revenue and income have grown over a period of several years, it's time to turn your attention to the profit and operating margins. These margins will take into account the company's costs and will give you a better idea of how it may perform in the future. It's important to know the difference between a profit and an operating margin. A profit margin is determined by a company's net income, which is after taxes. An operating margin is determined by the company's operating income, which is prior to taxes. Any significant changes in one margin and not the other could identify a change in the amount paid in taxes or

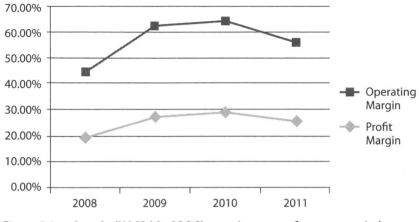

Figure 5.2   **Google (NASDAQ: GOOG) margins over a four year period.**

some other type of accounting change. Therefore, when I am comparing the operating and profit margins over a long period of time, I look for consistency between the two margins.

We have already established that Google is growing both in revenue and net income, but what is interesting is that Google's margins declined from 2010 to 2011, with a steep decline in operating margins (Figure 5.2). Prior to 2010, the company's margins had improved year over year, but they did slow gradually between 2009 and 2010. This could be an indication of a long-term problem. One year of declining margins is not enough to abandon a potential investment, but it definitely should be noted. If it continues over a period of several years, it probably means that spending is exceeding revenue, and the effectiveness of the company is regressing. Therefore, the company may not be best suited for a long-term investment until we identify some level of stability.

QUARTERLY PROGRESS

In addition to using a company's full-year progress, its quarterly progress should be charted as well. When comparing a company's quarterly progress, you can't compare the first quarter with the second quarter; you must compare year over year. For example, quarter 4 (Q4) of 2011 should be compared with Q4 of 2010. Seasonal peaks for companies in certain industries cause them to perform better during certain quarters. It wouldn't be accurate to compare the third- and fourth-quarter results of Sears because the company posts such large sales during its fourth-quarter holiday season. You could, however, compare the revenue, earnings, and margins of the fourth quarter for each of the last few years; this would determine whether or not the company is growing, along with the margin that it is growing.

JUST REMEMBER

As I begin to discuss fundamentals, which can become very confusing, my goal is to simplify the process so that you can make good investment decisions without becoming overwhelmed. As I end each section, I will reiterate the most important information that you should use while considering making an investment.

An income statement contains the most important data for analyzing a stock's immediate trend. When a company announces earnings and trades above or below a range, it's most likely because of its top- or bottom-line growth. Therefore, when you are choosing an investment, you need to compare the company's performance year over year in revenue and net income.

It's pointless for you to consume yourself with every number on an income statement. One of the most important things you need to consider is how fast the company is growing and whether the margins are sustained or improving over a period of time. A company's margins will give you other information that you will need from an income statement. It will give you an idea of how much the company is paying in taxes, its total costs, and how much it is spending to create additional revenue. Also, beware of any one-time special items on an income statement that may affect margins and earnings for a particular quarter. Do not use this as a reflection of the company's quarter but rather subtract the special item and then identify the company's income prior to the large cost. An income statement is very important in finding a good value investment, but it's only one piece of the puzzle. As we progress, read over and familiarize yourself with any metric you don't understand. If you need a term explained further, refer to investopedia.com, a reference site that is filled with definitions and explanations of investing terms and phrases.

CHAPTER 6

Balance Sheet and Cash Flow: The Keys to Long-Term Success

The stock market is filled with individuals who know the price of everything, but the value of nothing.

—PHILLIP FISHER

A FORGOTTEN MEASURE

The balance sheet and cash flow of a company sometimes are overlooked in the scheme of investing, but arguably, they are the most important data when you are considering a long-term investment. The level of importance you place on these two financial statements ultimately and directly will be related to your individual goals. Most short-term investors are much more consumed with the performance of an income statement, but long-term investors care more about a company's balance sheet and cash flow rather than short-term progress.

Unfortunately, the benefits of a company's strength in these two areas are rarely discussed, perhaps because it's not quite as exciting as revenue and income growth. If you have a time horizon beyond five years, you may want to pay attention to this aspect of investing and know that it's quite easy to find a financially strong company at a bargain price.

I place a high level of importance on a company's balance sheet and cash flow. A balance sheet can provide valuable information, such as a company's cash position, its leverage, and its amount of debt and liabilities. A company with a strong balance sheet is well positioned for growth through acquisitions and expansions. Meanwhile, a company with a weak balance sheet is at risk of bankruptcy in times of economic trouble and has limited long-term growth potential.

BALANCE SHEET

A balance sheet can provide valuable information, such as a company's cash position, its leverage, and its amount of debt and liabilities. A company with a strong balance sheet is well positioned for growth through acquisitions and expansions. Meanwhile, a company with a weak balance sheet is at risk of bankruptcy in times of economic trouble and has limited long-term growth potential. The information on a balance sheet should be vital to your investment strategy, and now let's talk about some of the key metrics and how they can be used to find a solid investment.

Cash

The first piece of information that you want to identify is the amount of *cash* a company has on its balance sheet. Then you want to look for trends, much as with revenue and income. You want to compare the cash position of a company year over year to make sure that its cash is increasing. If not, you should know why the cash position has stagnated or declined. If a company makes a large acquisition, its cash position could decline, and if it makes a fairly substantial expansion to produce more revenue for the future, its cash position also may decline. Sometimes a company will use its cash position to improve quarterly results or make changes to other areas of its balance sheet. Therefore, you need to be aware of how much cash the company whose stock you own has on its balance sheet over a given period of time.

Assets

An *asset* is a resource that a company owns to increase its value. Some assets will be useful or profitable for a balance sheet, whereas others may negatively display the strength of the balance sheet. I always tell people to look at a company's assets in a similar manner to their own assets, such as if you own a car and a house, those are your assets. Your car can be used as a way to get a loan, create cash, or provide transportation so that you can make additional money. Therefore, the car is an asset that is valuable to you as an individual and your ability to earn additional money.

A publically traded company's assets can be very complex, especially if you try to untangle all of the company's properties in an attempt to determine which assets are hurting and which assets are helping the company. I used the example of owning a car to explain what an asset is, but what happens if you paid too much for the car, it has lost some of its value, and now you can't afford the car? If you are in this situation, and let's say you have an outrageous mortgage, a boat, and a timeshare that you can't afford, then the assets become "toxic," greatly minimizing your ability to prosper.

A good example of assets turning toxic occurred during the housing crash of 2008. In fact, the term *toxic assets* was created during the housing crisis, explaining that the assets owned by the banks were hurting their performance. Banks were basically writing mortgages with their eyes closed and gave out too many loans to people who could not afford them. This practice, resulting in a domino effect, almost crashed our entire financial system. Too many defaults in too short of a time span caused an unpleasant situation in which banks could no longer afford the loss. This example, unfortunately, can become a reality very quickly. It's the investor's job to take into consideration other data on a balance sheet, such as liabilities, debt, cash, and equity, to ensure that the company whose stock you are purchasing is financially strong and hasn't taken on too much risk.

Liabilities

Liabilities are debts such as loans, mortgages, accrued expenses, and accounts payable that are documented on a balance sheet. These are debts that a company owes to another entity. There are two forms: current and long-term liabilities. *Current liabilities* are debts that are payable within one year, whereas *long-term liabilities* allow a longer period of time for repayment. Obviously, this gives investors some insight into any significant upcoming payments, as well as any large debts that will hinder the company's growth over the long term.

Equity

The *equity* of a company is its retained earnings and the amount of funds generated by shareholders. Equity also can be any asset that does not have any debt. While discussing assets, I gave the example of owning a car, which is an asset regardless of whether or not you owe money on it. However, a car becomes a person's equity once all debt against the car is paid. Now you have the ability to sell the property for cash without having any liabilities attached to the property. Now view this in relation to companies. While most companies have assets, which have some value attached, equity has value but does not put any financial strain on the company whatsoever. The amount of equity that a company has on its balance sheet often should be compared with its assets and debt to conclude how vulnerable the company may be in case of an unpredicted economic crisis.

USING A BALANCE SHEET AS A BASIS
TO MAKE AN INVESTMENT

Much like an income statement, there are several aspects to a balance sheet that have not been discussed. The key areas of a balance sheet are a company's assets, equity, debt, liabilities, and total amount of cash. My thoughts regarding one's ability to analyze a balance sheet are similar to those when analyzing an income statement. Understanding the terminology and knowing how to interpret data are very important, but you also should know that there is certain information that sums up the remaining data. With that being said, let's take a look at how you can use your knowledge of a balance sheet to make a better investment decision.

Now that you know the components of a balance sheet, you need to know how to use them to make better investment decisions. The first and most obvious move is to compare the data over a period of years, similar to an income statement. You want assets, cash, and equity to be rising or sustained and debt and liabilities to be falling. More specifically, you want to create and look for certain ratios and percentages within a balance sheet to sum up its information. The first set of information that is most meaningful to me on a balance sheet is a company's return on both equity and assets.

- **Return on equity.** This is a company's net income divided by shareholder's equity. This measure can be good when comparing similar companies in the same industry to see which company turns the most equity into profit. This can indicate a strong balance sheet.
- **Return on assets.** This is a company's net income divided by its total assets. This measures the efficiency of management using assets to return income. The return on assets is very important to me as a value investor because it shows the level of return that management can provide with an investment. However, like return on equity, it is best used when comparing like industries.

Regardless of which news provider you use, whether it be Yahoo, Google, Bloomberg, CNBC, Daily Finance, or your online broker, chances are that the news provider will list a company's return on both equity and assets over a period of time. I prefer Google Finance because I believe that it is the easiest to operate and shows detailed charts along with numbers. The following list shows you exactly how to view a company's balance sheet, cash flow, and income statement using Google Finance:

1. The first step is to visit Google.com.
2. When you are on Google's homepage, click the tab entitled "More" at the top of the page. You should see a variety of options, such as "Translate," "Books," "Scholar," etc. You also should see a tab entitled "Finance." If you do not see "Finance," then click "Even more," which is located within the "More" tab. Then you should be able to locate Google Finance.
3. After you have found Google Finance and you are on its homepage, you can search for a company. You want to type the company name (e.g., Microsoft) or its ticker symbol (e.g., MSFT), and it will take you to the company's homepage.
4. Once the company's homepage comes up, you will see a chart in the middle that shows the stock's trend. This chart displays the stock's trend at different times of the day or over a period of days, months, or years, making it interactive. Below the chart you will see a list of similar companies and a brief description of each company. Most important, though, on the left side you will see several tabs, one being "Financials," which you want to click on. This will take you to a page where you can see the company's fundamentals both on a chart and by the numbers.
5. Finally, as you are looking at the financials, you will have three different choices displayed at the top, for which

you can choose: the income statement, the balance sheet, and cash flow. You also can view the information over the last five quarters or over the last five years. It is good to review both the company's quarterly performance and the trend of its fundamentals year over year. Google Finance is helpful because its charts allow you to see the long- and short-term performance of a company's fundamentals and how the company compares over different time periods. Just remember, when comparing quarterly fundamentals, always make sure that you are comparing the same quarter but different years because the analysis will be irrelevant if you try to compare a first quarter with a second quarter. You need to see how the company performs year over year.

The information in this list can be found when viewing any fundamental measure. I think that it is important to know where to find the easiest places to compare information, in particular, the ratios and margins on an income statement or balance sheet. Now that you understand where to find this information, let's continue with the return on equity and assets (which both can be found on Google Finance).

The percentages that investors prefer for returns on assets and equity differ. There is no set standard of return that makes a company a good investment. It really depends on the industry and other components of the balance sheet. Some communication companies may have low single-digit returns, whereas other technology companies may have 20 percent returns on both assets and equity. All I care about is that the company is returning a positive amount on both its assets and equity, but I don't necessarily care what the percentage is that it returns. If a company returns a positive amount on its equity and assets, this tells me that the company is making good investment decisions and is well protected. Any company that is losing money on its investments is a company that is making bad decisions, reflecting a lack of management effectiveness.

Debt to Assets

The second area that I look at on a company's balance sheet is the ratio of debt to assets. It's very simple to calculate. If a company has $1 billion in assets and $250 million in debt, then it has a *debt-to-assets ratio* of 25 percent. You must take into consideration that certain industries typically operate with higher debt and lower assets. You want to compare similar companies because you may like one company because of its growth but realize that it carries much more debt than its competition, making its growth very dangerous.

A company's debt should be reflected as some form of assets. When you are finding a company's debt-to-assets ratio, you are seeing what percentage of the company's assets are liabilities. Therefore, I would not invest in a company that has more than 50 percent of its assets having debt or has a debt-to-assets ratio over 50 percent. Remember, the higher the ratio, the more significant is the risk because a company with a significant amount of debt is not positioned to deal with a large amount of adversity. Therefore, to be safe, stick to companies that have the capital and leverage to grow and deal with any issues that may arise.

Current Ratio

Much like a company's debt-to-assets ratio and its return on assets and equity, you won't find the current ratio written out on a company's balance sheet. The goal of using these percentages, ratios, or margins is to gain the maximum amount of information with the least amount of numbers, making research simpler.

The *current ratio* is found by taking the total number of current assets (assets with less than one year of life) and dividing them by the total number of current liabilities (a company's debt or obligations that are due within one year). Both the current assets and the current liabilities can be found on the company's balance sheet.

In theory, value investors prefer a larger current ratio of at least 2.0 or above. The goal of finding the current ratio is to determine a company's ability to meet its short-term obligations. Therefore, a higher ratio suggests a stronger financial position and an ability to pay off its debt. A current ratio under 2.0 doesn't necessarily mean that a company is in financial trouble, but it suggests that the company could face problems in the event of a financial crisis or economic downturn. (This is one of the key areas of research when seeking long-term investments.)

Cash Flow

The *cash flow* tells you where the company obtains its cash, the areas of its operation that return the largest amounts of cash, and its overall cash position. A company with a strong cash position is able to invest the cash into the business, which will increase the growth of the company and produce higher profits. A strong, balanced cash flow is vital for success when combined with a healthy balance sheet.

WHAT TO KNOW ABOUT CASH FLOW

Unfortunately, investors rarely pay attention to a company's cash flow. It is definitely not the most popular of the three statements. In fact, it rarely gets mentioned. However, the cash flow of a company is very important to understand. As an investor, you need to know where the company whose stock you are buying earns its money. Investors who understand and pay attention to a company's cash flow are typically much less surprised when unexpected events happen, resulting in a quarterly loss. One reason is the truthfulness of cash flow and the level of difficulty for a company to use any accounting tricks to manipulate the cash-flow numbers. Cash flow could be the most solid and useful information in determining a company's current financial well-being.

Unlike my approach to a company's income statement and balance sheet, I do not use any particular measure or margin to determine an investment decision within the cash flow. The information is important to know, understand, and use in completing the research puzzle. Therefore, let me continue to introduce some of the more important terms and measures within the statement of cash flow that will make you a much better investor.

Operating Cash Flow

The *operating cash flow* is a major piece of this particular financial statement. It informs the public of the amount of cash generated from the operations of a company. This particular measure is popular in the analysis of a company because it can inform investors about how much cash the company is creating from its day-to-day operations. Sometimes a company can post a negative operating cash flow but have positive cash flow from financing or investments, therefore posting net income for a quarter. This can occur for several quarters, sometimes years, allowing a company to almost hide its ineffective operational strategy. Therefore, one of the first indicators I seek is how much cash the company is earning from day-to-day operations.

Free Cash Flow

The *free cash flow* is the cash generated after the money is spent that is required to maintain or expand a company's assets. A large amount of free cash flow tells investors that a company can pursue other ventures with ease in an attempt to grow. This can be tricky because a negative free cash flow may not be a true negative if a large purchase of some sort occurred during the measured time. When looking at cash flow, it's important to take into account any expenses that may have affected the numbers. However, the free cash flow is important and should be positive over a period of several years to suggest that a company operates with efficiency.

Cash From . . .

The final measure that I am going to discuss is where a company receives its money. Usually, when people see that a company has reported record revenue, they don't take the time to dig in and ask themselves where the money came from. This particular section on the statement of cash flow informs us of the provider of cash, whether it be financing, operations, or investments. Each of the three items can be found on the company's cash-flow statement.

Cash from financing is the flow of cash between the company and its owners or creditors. For example, it would be the amount a company spends on dividends or stock repurchases. This particular cash flow is good for investors and shows a company's willingness to give money back to its investors.

Cash from operating activities is the cash from a company's regular business activities. A company's cash is what ultimately pays the bills, and the money it accrues from operating its business is what keeps the lights on. Therefore, it should be important for you in knowing that the company is returning a positive cash flow from its day-to-day operations and that it is strong in this area.

The *cash from investing activities* is any changes in a company's cash position owing to gains or losses from investments. This final measure of where a company originates its cash completes the statement of cash flow. As an investor, you want a balanced return on all the company's operations and origins of cash. Understanding where the money comes from will give you an edge in the market because sometimes you can see the strength or weakness of a company before the market does or before it even reflects on a company's income statement. Remember, top- and bottom-line numbers on an income statement can be manipulated with accounting practices, but cash flow is not so easily altered. This can be a good indicator of whether or not you are buying into a good company.

JUST REMEMBER

If your goal is to become a successful long-term investor, you really want to pay close attention to a company's balance sheet and cash flow. Remember, the behavior of the market offers short-term gains, but the fundamentals are what will dictate the long-term movement of a stock. I consider the balance sheet and cash flow to be the most important information when deciding on whether or not to buy shares in a company. These items get overlooked because there are very few pieces of data from either statement that are incorporated as leading stock metrics. These statements give you valuable insight into the operations of a company that you don't get from an income statement.

As a value investor, my goal is to buy a stock that is fundamentally strong but is priced cheap. In order for its stock to be fundamentally strong, a company needs to be well capitalized, as well as being efficient and able to withstand any economic hardships. The only way for the balance sheet and cash-flow statements to be strong would be if the company is profitable from its assets and equity with measured returns on both. You also want a company with assets that outweigh its liabilities, so you need to seek a company with a debt-to-assets ratio far below 50 percent and compare two companies in the same industry (e.g., AT&T versus Verizon). Finally, you need to know the origin of the company's cash and which activities create the cash, and you must be on the lookout for any red flags (which I will discuss later).

This may seem overwhelming, but with a little practice, it will become much easier. I have laid out a company's income statement, balance sheet, and cash flow in the easiest manner that I know. Knowing and understanding the information and areas of these statements are only the beginning steps toward finding value in a company. I have shared with you not only the definition of each metric but also what to look for when searching for value. This information will help you as we proceed and will be important to your overall success as a value investor.

CHAPTER 7

Stock Metrics

Although it's easy to forget sometimes, a share is not a
lottery ticket . . . it's part-ownership of a business.

—PETER LYNCH

The idea behind being a value investor is kind of like hunting for
deer. When you hunt for a deer, you first go out and scout the best
possible areas in which the deer may wander. This is similar to the
research that is needed in finding a fundamentally strong company.
After you have found a good area for hunting deer or found several
fundamentally strong companies, you can move on to the next step.
The next step is patience, waiting for a deer to cross your carefully
selected path. This is very similar to investing because after you find
the fundamentally strong company, you have to wait for a value price
to present itself. However, like a hunter, you can pick the absolute
best spot and still have no luck. This is where investing differs: If
you found enough quality companies, it would be like having 20
hunters in good locations and only needing one deer.

You should by now have a clear perception of how to identify
a fundamentally strong company, so the next step is simply being

patient. In the final chapter of this section I am examining stock metrics, which aren't necessarily fundamentals, but they are derived from fundamentals. The metrics of a stock tell you when value is being presented by using the fundamentals and incorporating them into a metric that tells you whether or not a stock is priced too high or too low. I have spent an extra amount of time on this particular chapter so as to explain each metric with as much detail as possible. These metrics will be important as we proceed throughout this book in helping to identify and capitalize on value.

THE HOMEPAGE METRICS

If you were to go to any financial website such as Yahoo! Finance or Bloomberg and type in a particular stock name, you would be taken to its homepage. The company's homepage would include an assortment of basic information such as the stock price and metrics of the stock. These metrics will differ from site to site, but certain metrics are standard throughout all financial sites. I call these standard metrics the *homepage metrics* because they appear on just about every financial website's homepage for any particular stock. The homepage may include other metrics as well, but 95 percent of the time it will contain five metrics in particular.

Stock Price

Obviously, when you visit a company's homepage on any financial site, the first and largest piece of data is going to be the trading price of the stock. I will discuss the stock price of a company in great detail, but not until you have a better understanding of the information used for finding the price of a stock. For now, it's important to know that the price of a stock is irrelevant and means nothing in terms of value or worth of a particular company. For example, if Sirius XM is priced at $2.50 a share, it does not mean that it is worth the same as JA Solar Holdings, even if both stocks are priced the same. Some people are easily confused by the price of a stock and believe that a stock's price reflects its total worth. Theoretically, a company that is worth $200 billion can be worth $2 per share if the company issues 100 billion shares. The price has nothing to do with the worth or value of a company, and a lower stock price does not necessarily mean that the shares will fluctuate with greater intensity. I will explain the valuation of a company in more detail as we progress, but it's important to know that the price of a stock can be misleading and doesn't reflect the valuation of a company.

Market Cap

The *market capitalization* (market cap), however, does dictate the worth of a company because it tells you the total value of the company according to the stock market. It is found by calculating the total number of outstanding shares issued by the company multiplied by the price of the stock. The market cap of a company is much more important than the price of the stock because it tells the investor how greatly the company is valued. For example, the following table shows three pretend companies and how market caps dictate the price of their stock.

MARKET CAP	TOTAL SHARES	STOCK PRICE
$500 million	5 million	$100
$500 million	50 million	$ 10
$500 million	100 million	$ 5

As you can see, each of the three companies has a market cap of $500 million, which means that this is what the market has valued each company. Because of the number of issued shares, the stock price is different. All three companies have equal worth but different stock prices. If you can afford the $5 stock, then you can purchase the $100 stock. It really makes no difference because you are buying a company that has equal worth.

With some investors, there is a deep psychological attachment to a $5 stock over a $50 stock, even if the companies are worth the same. The reason reflects a person's perception and belief that a cheaper stock will double or post gains in a shorter period of time. There is also a belief that an investor will own less of a company if the price is more expensive. These myths are incorrect because the price has nothing to do with performance. Just because a stock is cheaper doesn't mean that you own more; it simply means that the company issued more shares. However, it is normal and common that Wall Street and retail investors alike place a significant amount of emphasis on the price of a stock, I urge you to avoid the temptation.

One of my favorite books is *Fire Your Stock Analyst* by Harry Domash, and in the book he discusses a wide range of topics. Overall, I believe that his perception and mine fairly align on a number of critical issues regarding the market. However, one subject he talks about is the price of a stock by saying (paraphrase) that most stocks worth your attention are above $5. He says that stocks trading below that level are called *penny stocks* and that risk-averse investors won't touch them. Now, to be fair, he is referring to mostly stocks under $0.50 and he is discussing the games that are played on Wall Street to "promote" small companies with business practices that may or may not be legitimate. However, I strongly disagree with his opinions, and there are two points to be made from his comment.

The first point is that there is a major emphasis placed on the stock above "$5" because most funds can't touch them unless the price is above $5. Hence when he says that risk-averse investors won't touch them he is referring to the fact that funds won't buy stocks below the price. Therefore, the stock below $5 is typically more volatile, and doesn't have the same level of institutional support as a company above the $5 mark.

The second point is that it is not wise to judge a company's size based on its price; you must learn to judge its size by market capitalization. Alcatel-Lucent is currently a $1.20 stock, but is worth more than seven times the value of Travelzoo, a company with a price over $20. Bottom line: Don't fall into the trap of judging a company on its stock price—look at its fundamentals and its market cap and make a decision based on those factors.

Price-to-Earnings (P/E) Ratio

The *P/E ratio* of a stock is one of the value investor's best friends. It shows how high the stock is trading above the company's earnings over a 12-month period, and it tells you how expensive a stock is trading compared with its earnings. To explain how a P/E ratio can be useful to a value investor, I'll compare the valuation of two similar companies—Amazon and eBay—for the year 2011.

To find the P/E ratio of a company, we need two pieces of information: the net income for the last 12 months, in this case 2011, and the current market capitalization of the company. We can then take the market cap and divide the net income to find the P/E ratio of the company's stock.

COMPANY	MARKET CAP	NET INCOME	P/E RATIO
Amazon	$84 billion	$631 million	133
eBay	$48 billion	$3.229 billion	14.86

As you can see, Amazon has the higher P/E ratio by a very significant margin. According to the stock market, Amazon is worth nearly twice as much as eBay, but it posted just 20 percent above eBay in income in 2011. The level at which Amazon is trading suggests that it is a momentum stock and is not appropriately valued as a value investment. Furthermore, considering a company such as Amazon, I personally wouldn't buy the stock unless its P/E ratio was under 30 with a market cap of $20 billion.

There are several questions that you may be asking in regard to valuation after seeing the comparison between eBay and Amazon. Why is Amazon more expensive? Why does the market have it valued so high? Would Amazon or eBay make a good investment? First, there are several reasons why Amazon may be priced so high. It is our own personal obligation to find reason as to why it is priced so high and then decide if the stock is worth the high valuation. A stock may present an especially high valuation if it is growing at some unprecedented rate or if the company is being considered as an acquisition target. Since there could be several different reasons indicating a large valuation, it is your job to find the reason and see for yourself if its large valuation is validated.

The P/E ratio is of utmost importance to value investors because it is one of the first ways to compare the fundamental growth of a company with its valuation. As an investor, our first job is to find a company with strong fundamentals, which is not that difficult. However, it can be difficult to find a company that is appropriately valued.

There is no standard for a P/E ratio, but obviously a ratio of 133 is quite high. Some industries trade with higher P/E ratios than others; therefore, it's always a good idea to compare the ratios of similar companies, such as Amazon and eBay. You then must determine an appropriate price based on the company's growth. The P/E ratio is not a "tell all" indicator, but if you've already found a company that interests you and has an attractive P/E ratio, then you are on the right track.

As I mentioned earlier, there are no written rules of buying a stock with a P/E ratio that is too high; it all depends on the industry, the company, its growth, and so on. There are so many factors that go into deciding whether or not a stock is presenting value that you shouldn't give any one ratio or stock metric priority. However, I try to follow a certain guideline, which is based on a company's earnings-per-share (EPS) growth (bottom-line growth) and a P/E ratio that I feel is appropriate based on the company's year-over-year income growth.

BOTTOM-LINE GROWTH	MAXIMUM P/E RATIO PER GROWTH
5 percent	≥9
10 percent	≥13
15 percent	≥17
20 percent	≥21
25 percent	≥25
30 percent	≥31
40 percent	≥45

This table is not perfect, and of course, there are exceptions to this rule. Later, in Part IV, I will elaborate on this chart and show you how to incorporate other factors into a formula for finding appropriate value. I have always tried to stay true to this chart while buying stocks based on P/E ratios, although certain situations may present themselves so that you deviate from your plan, and that's okay. There is no one standard method that is correct.

As you may notice, the numbers change according to the level of growth. If a company is growing its bottom line by 15 percent year over year, I personally am not willing to buy a stock that may be trading above 17 times earnings. When a company is growing by 40 percent year over year, I would be willing to test a P/E ratio of 40. The key is finding fast-growing companies that fit into a category based on how you assess value.

The P/E ratio of a stock is very important to value investors and is one of the first stock metrics that is noticed by investors. A high or low P/E ratio should not determine whether or not a stock would make a good investment. It is definitely important to identify and should be one of the many tools in the shed, so to speak, in helping you to identify a fundamentally strong company, one that is trading at a price that has existing value.

Volume

Volume is a measure of the total number of shares, or contracts, that change hands in a particular trading day. It is a metric that is measured in two ways: average volume and daily volume. The *average volume* measures the number of shares traded on a daily basis for a period of three months, and the *daily volume* is the number of shares traded for a particular day. Together these two measures may not help you in making an investment decision, but they can help you to identify the direction of a stock, which could result in value.

This particular measure is more popular among technical traders (those who rely on chart indicators) than among fundamentalists. It is a major indicator for technical traders because it shows differences in conviction among investors or a change in momentum. Because we are value investors, this can be very important because our job is to find not only a fundamentally strong company but also one that is satisfactorily priced to buy.

The trend of volume is a topic that I am going to discuss in great detail as we enter into behavioral finance because it is a very broad topic. Investors who use volume as one of their primary indicators entertain the notion that major increases and declines in daily volume will validate a change in direction of a stock. For example, let's say that Sprint trades 50 million shares on average and is priced at $3.50 a share. If the stock were to trade 200 million shares the following day and close at $3.40, some investors might suggest that it may trade lower for the next few days (or longer). The same can be said if the same stock were to rise to $3.90 when 200 million shares are traded. Some would suggest that it may continue to trade higher.

Those who trade according to a stock's day-to-day volume pay attention to every little change. They look for any movement and compare it with the price of the stock. Their theory is that when volume jumps and the stock changes direction, investors are committing to the buy or sell. However, like most technical beliefs, it contradicts itself and fails more times than it succeeds. There are too many other factors involved for a stock's direction to be determined by one day of high volume. It could be caused by the initial reaction after an earnings report or some other unknown key development. It could be a domino effect, with investors buying or selling to take profits or to avoid additional loss, with a plan to sell or buy back at a later time. I don't believe that it is possible to determine the immediate direction of a stock (day to day), but I do believe that volume can be important in helping you to identify the momentum of a stock over a longer period of time. With technical indicators, there is simply too much room for error because the indicators all contradict each other. On a day-to-day basis you have a 50 percent chance of guessing a stock's direction, and I don't believe that this is influenced by any chart (because investors are not logical). However, you can identify whether or not the stock is cheap based on fundamentals and whether it presents the likelihood of trading higher over a period of time.

Beta

The *beta* of a stock is a good way to help assess the risk in an investment. Beta is a measure of volatility in a stock compared with the market. Let me explain: The market is measured with a beta of 1.0, which reflects its volatility. It is 1.0 because all other beta measures are based on its beta of 1.0. Therefore, it doesn't matter how volatile the market trades, the beta will always be 1.0.

Every stock has a beta, and its beta is its measure of volatility compared with the market. For example, let's say a stock has a beta of 0.35, which means that the stock is 35 percent as volatile as the market. This would indicate that the stock does not move with the market or by the same degree when the market trades higher or lower. Theoretically, the market may increase by 1 percent on any given day, yet the stock with a beta of 0.35 would only increase 0.35 percent, which works the same during a down market. These numbers aren't exact, but they are an average of performance and can help investors who want to limit risk.

There are certain industries that trade with less volatility than others. If you decide that you want to be safe, utility stocks, which are low-beta and high-yield investments, are popular choices. However, some investors choose banking stocks such as Bank of America, which trades with a beta of over 2.0 (meaning that the stock is 100 percent more volatile than the market). This gives an investor a better chance for large gains, but you have to be confident in the direction of the market because of its volatility.

Beta is one of the more popular metrics of the day for swing traders, but it also should be used by value investors to determine a security's movement compared with the market. Like the four metrics I have already discussed, it is one of the five metrics that is seen on nearly all financial websites. You can find the beta by visiting any financial website and entering the ticker symbol for a particular stock. Most likely the beta will be listed on the company's homepage beside the other four metrics that I have already discussed.

THE LESS POPULAR BUT STILL IMPORTANT METRICS

There are probably hundreds of potential metrics that can be found for a particular stock. You can find and compare nearly any fundamental measure with the valuation of a stock. Stock metrics are important because they tell you how a company is valued in terms of an investment, and they also summarize several fundamental measures. The following metrics are much less discussed among investors but are of utmost importance in making an investment decision. Remember, you can find the perfect company, but if it is valued too high, your gains will be limited, or you could return a loss. The following metrics should be incorporated into your research after finding a fundamentally strong company to ensure that you are buying a stock that is "cheap" based on its fundamentals.

Enterprise Value

The *enterprise value* of a company is a different way to value a company rather than using market capitalization. It is much less popular and rarely discussed among investors, but it takes debt into account when determining the valuation of a company. Remember that a market cap is the value of a company according to the market, based on its earnings per share (EPS), outstanding shares, and P/E ratio. The enterprise value of a company still takes into account the valuation of the company according to the market, but it incorporates the company's debt, minority interest and preferred shares (which both have to do with ownership), and its cash position. Thus a better way to find value of a company is by noticing a large differentiation in the valuation of the company's market cap and enterprise value.

The enterprise value of a company can be difficult to calculate and is not one of the five primary metrics on a company's homepage. Therefore, you need to know how to find the number that will reduce the amount of time involved in comparing these metrics. Some investors may tell you that it is important to know how to determine a company's value, and although I agree, I believe that it's just as useful in understanding value and knowing where to find it, so you can research other areas. I ask that you examine the following guide, which will walk you through how to find each of the less popular but important metrics. It will show you how to find each of the metrics that are discussed on the Internet in the easiest possible way.

1. Visit Yahoo.com, and choose the "Finance" site from its list of many sites.
2. When you are on the homepage of Yahoo! Finance, you will see a box near the top of the page entitled "Get quotes." Type the name of a company, say, "Apple," or enter the ticker symbol of the company, say, "AAPL," to visit its homepage.
3. After visiting the homepage, you will notice each of the five homepage metrics that I have already discussed, but to find the others, you must search within the tabs on the homepage. On the left-hand side, you will see a variety of tabs. Choose the tab entitled "Key statistics."
4. When you arrive in the "Key statistics" area, you will notice a variety of information. This information includes the margins, percentages, and metrics that I have already discussed and others that will be discussed.
5. Aside from "Key statistics," you will notice other important tabs, such as "Financials," "Analyst opinions," and "Key developments." These areas should be explored because they will help you toward making a better investment decision, especially now that you're more knowledgeable about the terminology.

Forward P/E Ratio

The *forward P/E ratio* is very similar to the P/E ratio, but it's a prediction of what the stock's P/E ratio will be in the future, one year after earnings. Remember, a P/E ratio is very important to investors and is used as an indicator of value. It shows how the market prices a stock compared with its earnings (or EPS). A forward P/E ratio is based on expectations because it takes the current valuation and finds a P/E ratio based on analysts' expectations for the following year's earnings. To better understand, take a look at the following chart.

EPS	TOTAL SHARES	P/E RATIO	MARKET CAP
$1.25	100 million	20	$2.5 billion

This chart illustrates our starting point of a stock and will be used to find the forward P/E ratio. It is important to remember that with a forward P/E ratio, all information stays the same, with the exception of the EPS. The goal is to determine a stock's EPS if it were trading with its current metrics but with next year's earnings.

Let's say that the analysts expect our pretend company to earn $155 million next year. There are several ways to flip-flop the numbers to find the forward P/E ratio, but the easiest way is to simply divide the market cap by the expected income.

$2.5 billion / $155 million = 16.13 (forward P/E)

Now that we have our forward P/E ratio of 16.13, let's talk about what it means. First, we know that analysts expect the company's earnings to grow. For a company that is expected to grow by nearly 25 percent, its forward ratio is pretty attractive (according to the earlier chart that showed value and P/E ratios). The most important point to remember is that a lower forward P/E ratio means that analysts expect the company to grow, and a higher ratio means that earnings are expected to decline. There are several ways to use this when making an investment decision. If a company constantly outperforms earnings expectations, its future ratio may be much smaller than analysts expect, which could mean additional value.

The forward P/E ratio is one of the most important metrics to a value investor because it takes into account future earnings and the value of a company. Since the market trades according to future expectations, this could be the best indicator of all metrics. I have shown you how to calculate this metric, but since it can be found under the "Key statistics" tab on Yahoo! Finance, you don't have to take the time trying to find a company's following year expectations or calculating what the forward P/E ratio may be. You know how to find it, and now you understand its purpose. Because you are a value investor, this is one of the many tools that must be in the shed while attempting to identify a fundamentally strong company that is trading with value-presenting metrics. Since market trades are based on future expectations, this is a good indication of the future trend of a stock.

Price/Sales Ratio

The *price/sales ratio* of a company can be found just like the rest of the stock metrics, by visiting the "Key statistics" page on Yahoo! Finance. It is a very simple metric to find because it's exactly like the P/E ratio. Instead of using a company's net income, you use its revenue (or sales). The metric tells you how expensive the stock is compared with its total revenue, which is important to value investors.

This metric is important when you are comparing similar companies. For example, even though Walmart and Google have $200 billion market caps, indicating an equal level of worth, the two companies have complete different price/sales ratios.

COMPANY	MARKET CAP	REVENUE	PRICE/SALES RATIO
Walmart	$200 billion	$447 billion	0.47
Google	$200 billion	$37.90 billion	5.33

Both Walmart and Google have similar valuations but return different levels of revenue. The difference is reflected as the price/sales ratio, which shows that Walmart is cheaper compared with its total revenue. However, you can't compare the price/sales ratio of a technology company with that of a retail company. The comparison must be between companies of the same industry because retail companies typically have higher revenue and lower margins than a technology company. Either way, the price/sales ratio is a metric that must be used in addition to a company's P/E ratio. It's one of the best ways to find companies that are priced cheaply, and it's a metric that is rarely discussed.

Price/Earnings to Growth Ratio

The *price/earnings to growth ratio (PEG ratio)* of a stock is another metric in the class of P/E ratio and forward P/E ratio. Its purpose is to determine whether a stock is overvalued according to its expected EPS growth. The use of this ratio is very similar to that of a forward P/E ratio. All things considered, a lower number means more value. The PEG ratio is preferred by a large number of investors because, as a metric, it shows a level of expected growth.

Float

Float is best explained by the number of shares (or percentage) of a company's total shares that are traded in the market. A company may have 500 million total shares, but it may only trade 100 million shares in the market. A rule of thumb is that the smaller the float, the more volatile is the stock. The size of the float is important to day traders and those with short-term horizons because stocks with small floats move much more easily compared with those with larger floats. The size of the float is relevant to a value investor during the assessment of risk for a particular stock.

Short Interest

Over the last five years there have been countless books written about complex option strategies that *can* be used to make money with less risk. In this book, I purposely avoided the discussion of options. The reason is because it is complex and can be very dangerous for investors who are new to handling their own finances. With the markets already being difficult, there is no reason to complicate it further with additional information that is also complex. However, in order to help you with buying a stock at the right time, it's beneficial for you to understand *short interest* and also a *short interest ratio*, but not to use either as the primary decision maker for when to buy a stock.

The short interest of a stock is not hard to find. You can locate it on almost all company pages on a financial website. And it is the percentage of outstanding shares that are held short. When someone "shorts" a stock, they are buying it and expecting it to fall, therefore they make money when and if the stock falls lower. I view short interest as a sentiment indicator; it tells me what direction investors expect a stock to trend in the immediate future. If a stock has a short interest of 2 percent, then there are not many people betting that it will fall lower. If the stock has a short interest of 10 percent, then it may not be best time to buy, because when and if the stock begins to fall, it will fall aggressively as the lower targets are hit.

The short-interest ratio is another indicator that is easy to find and tells you the length of time it will take investors who are shorting a stock to "cover" their position if the stock begins to rise. If a stock's short-interest ratio is low, then it tells the investor that the stock could rally fairly quickly. However, a short-interest ratio above six may indicate that a rally could reverse quickly and a stock could trade lower.

My goal is to spend the least amount of time as possible discussing topics related to options, but in this "trader market," which means fewer long-term investors and more day-to-day traders, the use of options is becoming more and more popular. As an opportunistic investor, the short-interest and short-interest ratio are two metrics that should be monitored in order to buy at the best price. To make it easy, try to avoid stocks with a short-interest and a short-interest ratio above five. Of course, if a stock has fallen and there is great value in the stock, then it would trump a short-interest above five and you should buy the stock. And although short-interest is not the most important metric, it is still something to monitor.

Ownership

It is common that as you are collecting the data on a company/stock, you will hear a lot of chatter about the ownership of the company. Obviously, a traded company on one of the large exchanges is considered a public company, owned by investors. However, investors like to keep in mind institutional versus insider ownership. This information can be found on many financial websites, or for more details, you can search for a company's ownership on the Securities and Exchange Commission (SEC) website, which provides all the details about the publically traded company because all information must be reported. More specifically, a company's 13D filing with the SEC shows large transactions.

If a company has large insider ownership, then managers and those within the company own shares. As an investor, I always look for companies that have strong insider ownership. My theory is that large insider ownership is a sign of faith among those who make decisions because, think about it, would you really want to own a company in which those who control the company avoid owning it?

Institutional ownership reflects the shares owned by hedge, mutual, and pension funds, along with other institutions. Along with large insider ownership, it can provide stability to the price of the stock, that is, unless a large investor decides to dump shares. Then you could have large losses. For the most part, though, it's better to have more institutional ownership than less. Remember that these institutions have resources that aren't available to the everyday retail investor because companies want their business. I will say to be careful about buying shares "just because" of prominent investors such as Carl Icahn or Warren Buffett. The market loves when high-profile investors buy shares in a company, but because you don't know when such buyers bought shares or the terms of their purchase, it can be dangerous to simply buy because someone else bought.

PUTTING IT TOGETHER

Here's a fact: You could spend hours on hours of due diligence locating countless measures of fundamental data. I have simplified the process and listed what I believe to be the most important areas of a company's fundamentals and the metrics of its stock. This information is vital to the remainder of this book because it is all based on the information that we have discussed. Now you are ready to learn how to become an opportunistic investor, that is, once you've identified a fundamentally strong company.

The most significant problem with the data that I have presented is that it tells an incomplete story. I have simply selected distinct sections of what I feel is most important and provides you with the most information. I have asked you to familiarize yourself with the terms; your knowledge and understanding of such will enable you to make a wise investment decision. My goal is to make investing easier for you, but I am sure the terminology and examples do not seem so easy thus far. How can you use all the information and terms that I have discussed in order to make a better investment decision? So as to not be overwhelmed, for now, all I want is for you to understand the terminology and the basics behind the metrics of a stock.

I have discussed the income statement, balance sheet, cash flow, and 10 metrics that I believe are most useful. Now it is time to put it all together. Unfortunately, there is no right or wrong way to incorporate the information that I have given you—and no way to guarantee large return (which is why no one has a 100 percent success rate). There is a way, however, to incorporate the information and allow you to make much better decisions that will return an overall gain, which I know will make you more than happy.

In Chapter 8, I will be putting the information together, which should help you to make more advantageous investment decisions.

You will need to know the definitions, or the basic meanings, of the terms that I have discussed in the last three chapters to understand the outline that I provide, which should provide you with the conception of how to incorporate this information. I am sure that this may seem a bit overwhelming at the moment, but I really want to help you learn how to find a fundamentally strong company with great metrics. In Chapter 8, I will also show you how you can be successful at identifying these traits. Then I will proceed into the next part, discussing the true characteristic of a successful value investor, who is a person of patience and opportunity who uses the craziness of the market to find value and buy stocks at their cheapest prices for the largest possible gains.

Using Fundamentals to Make an Investment Decision

Know what you own, and know why you own it.

—PETER LYNCH

By now I have filled your brain with so much information that you probably feel a little despaired. Unfortunately, this bewilderment is a necessary state of being in the world of investing. It is really not my goal to confuse you when it comes to investing, but the truth is that there are no written rules and no way to invest with any level of success without knowing the basic information, which can seem somewhat overwhelming in the beginning.

Thus far I have provided basic information concerning the three primary financial statements and given insight into how they are incorporated into a stock's valuation. The question that remains is how to use the information in making better investment decisions. There are several steps to follow that will answer this question. Keep in mind that these steps have nothing to do with when to buy or anything related to behavioral finance. At this point, you are simply using the information that we have already discussed to help you identify a fundamentally strong company with attractive metrics. The goal is to simplify the information in a way that can be useful when making an investment decision.

SIMPLIFYING BY GOALS

The easiest way I know to simplify the information is to break it down by goals. Throughout this entire book I have discussed goals and having a clear idea of what you want to accomplish as an investor. This is extremely important because no two people have the exact same goals. Your goal may be to invest as a long-term investor, but you may not be in the best financial position to do that because you may need to sell at any given point for a personal expense. You may be investing to pay for your children's college tuition or to earn extra money for a down payment on a home. Regardless of your reasons, you have decided that investing may be your best opportunity to get a return of significant cash. The time allotment allowed and the best strategy for earning the cash will differ.

Unfortunately, I cannot break down every reason that someone may choose to invest, nor can I give you a personalized plan based on your own investment goals. This is one of the reasons why it is good to at least consult with a financial advisor, one who will guide you in the right direction. However, based on my experience, investors fall into one of three categories: situational trader, short-term investor, or a long-term investor.

You may not know which category best describes you, or you may know exactly which category in which you belong. The characteristics of these three types may help you to determine which investing style may be most appropriate for you. A person who is a situational trader doesn't invest the same as a long-term investor, nor does she place the same level of emphasis on the same metrics. It would seem that the best way to put the fundamental information that I have discussed into action is to allocate the information according to investment strategy. Then you can develop your own mental image as to why certain indicators are more important to specific investors.

SITUATIONAL TRADER

A *situational trader* is neither a long- nor short-term investor but rather trades stocks to achieve a purpose. The purpose may be to ride the momentum, buy before earnings, or trade the market's volatility so as to return larger gains. Those who act with this "get rich quick" philosophy are more concerned with a stock's current position and any differentiation in momentum rather than fundamentals.

My purpose is to not discourage or spend time talking about the negatives of this philosophy. However, I think the purpose is obvious: It compares more to a game of blackjack than to investing. You have a 50/50 chance of determining the immediate trend or day-to-day trend of a stock. A situational trader tries to create a strategy or a science behind identifying the day-to-day trend of a stock.

Let's say that you are a situational trader. In order to find a stock that presents an immediate upside, you would be more concerned with stock metrics than fundamental measures. If your goal is to capitalize on the immediate trend of a stock, which of the metrics and/or information I have discussed would be the most relevant to you (see Table 8.1)?

Table 8.1   **Concerns of a Situational Trader**

MOST CONCERNED	LEAST CONCERNED
Float	Balance sheet
Beta	Cash flow
Volume	Forward ratios
Price/earnings (P/E) ratio	Price/sales ratio
Top and bottom line	Income statement analysis

The situational trader is not concerned with the fundamental analysis needed to make a good investment decision because, after all, he is only concerned about the immediate trend. Therefore, there is little analysis of a company's balance sheet and cash flow because situational traders believe that they have little effect on the immediate trend. Instead, situational traders are mostly concerned with the measures that have the potential to move a stock for the greater amount of an immediate upside.

To a situational trader, the float is an important metric because it tells how many shares are available for trading. A small float indicates that a stock could move higher (or lower) with minimal news or developments. Therefore, a situational trader wants a stock with a relatively low float.

The beta tells the situational trader how volatile a stock trades compared with the market, so it would be important for traders who seek large movement. It makes sense that a situational trader would want a stock that trades more volatile than the market because a high beta and a low float equal a stock that could trade higher when given any kind of catalyst, regardless of how small.

A significant change in volume indicates a change in investor conviction, which can be an indicator of short-term movement. A large percentage of investors pays attention to this metric and relies on variations to indicate a change in direction. This is sometimes the first metric that attracts the situational trader and indicates that movement may occur.

The P/E ratio is a universal metric that is used by all investors to determine a stock's valuation compared with its earnings. It is important to traders because it reflects the market's expectations for a company. A high ratio indicates that the market expects higher earnings, and a lower ratio indicates low expectations. A value investor will usually seek low ratios in companies that are inaccurately valued, but a situational trader may seek a stock that is trading with a high level of optimism or momentum regardless of value.

A large number of situational traders are people who play earnings. Therefore, the top- and bottom-line earnings for a company can be very important for a situational trader's expectations. The trader may buy a stock before or after earnings have exceeded expectations (causing the stock to react), especially if the stock trades with the remainder of the metrics, which is what is most important to the situational trader.

Some would suggest that the market is made up of 80 percent situational traders, and I would agree. The majority of investors is overly emotional, irrational, and makes illogical decisions when presented with the possibility of returning large gains in a short period of time. We are a society that demands immediate results, and we are sometimes fooled by the attractiveness of the measures that drive situational investors. We tend to overreact and sell or buy too quickly. Then we wonder why our portfolio suffers. The key is learning how to profit from this irrational behavior and stay true to the measures that will return consistent income. Therefore, you should think of a situational trader's analysis as a guide on what *not* to do. The chances of succeeding with any level of consistency are extremely low, but if you do, you should start trying your luck at your local casino.

SHORT-TERM INVESTOR

Some investors believe that a situational trader and a short-term investor have the same characteristics. The truth is actually to the contrary. A situational trader plays immediate trends and tries to capitalize on volatility or key developments—an active trader. A *short-term investor* has short-term goals, which usually are specific for the investment. For example, when I buy a stock with a short-term horizon, the stock usually does not pay a dividend, and I usually buy with the goal of not holding more than one year, usually less than six months or until my goal is reached. A short-term investor is usually an active investor but is not as active as a situational trader. This form of investing can be very successful if stocks are bought during a time of opportunity and are held throughout periods of volatility. The key to its success is eliminating emotion (see Table 8.2).

Table 8.2   **Concerns of a Short-Term Investor**

MOST CONCERNED	LEAST CONCERNED
Earnings growth	Cash flow
Margin growth	Taxes
P/E ratio	Long-term debt
Forward ratio	Volume
Price/sales ratio	Float
Some balance sheet	Yield

The fundamental analysis of an individual investor will differ from person to person. The preceding is simply a standard for which metrics may be most important to investors with different goals. This includes the first and last areas of research.

As you can see, the short-term investor and the situational trader do have some similarities. Neither, however, places a high level of importance on the cash flow of a company. The cash flow is perhaps the most ignored statement of income for a company, and for most short-term investors, it is typically overlooked. The cash flow will tell you where the company's money comes from. If the company is creating its cash from financing and has years of negative cash flow, this eventually could affect its quarterly performance. Yet, because it has minimal immediate impact on the stock, cash flow is overlooked for other metrics.

LONG-TERM INVESTOR

The goals and characteristics of a long-term investor should be self-explanatory. A *long-term investor* has the goal of building wealth over a period of many years. This approach typically is referred to as a *buy-and-hold strategy*. In order to become a successful long-term investor, you must be willing to weather the storm of the market's volatility and be capable of finding a company that will stand the test of time while continuing to grow and evolve over a period of many years (see Table 8.3).

Table 8.3   **Concerns of a Long-Term Investor**

MOST CONCERNED	LEAST CONCERNED
Cash flow	N/A
Balance sheet	N/A
Valuation	N/A
Earnings growth	N/A
History	N/A
Unmeasured fundamentals	N/A

You may first notice that there isn't any information in the "Least Concerned" column because most long-term investors are consumed with every measure of a company prior to buying its stock, which makes a great deal of sense. If you are going to buy a stock and plan to hold it for many years, you want to know that it is well positioned in every category.

The long-term investor pays close attention to the balance sheet and cash flow of a company. A situational and short-term holder can manage to ignore these two statements because any issues within either statement may not affect the company for many years. However, a long-term investor must be aware that the company returns strong gains on its equity and assets that meet industry standards, along with having an attractive debt-to-assets ratio (mostly under 20 percent). You want to know that the company has a large amount of cash and has a strong cash flow throughout its day-to-day operations. These areas are all very important, and once the long-term investor has found a company that meets the qualifications for a long-term investment, she must look at the valuation and possible return.

As a long-term investor, the last thing I want is to buy a stock that is near the top of its range. Too often investors will invest in a company long term and return minimal gains because the company trades with little movement and large yield. The key to investing in a good company is buying when it's cheap. That way you can buy more shares and return larger gains. As a result, the stock metrics and valuation of the company are very important. Therefore, you want to know its stock metrics and identify its trading pattern over a period of 10 years to determine what price is good to buy.

It is my personal belief that there are several equally great long-term investments. There are several companies with a great history that most likely will continue to grow. Therefore, I am not willing to buy shares in a company that is not "on sale." It makes no sense to buy a stock near the top of its range if you can buy another one that is equally successful at a much cheaper price with more upside.

YOU—THE FUNDAMENTAL INVESTOR

What are you? Are you a situational trader, a short- or long-term investor, or none of the above? I personally fall under the category of none of the above. I am somewhere between a short- and long-term investor. And honestly, the most successful investors don't limit themselves to being just one type of investor; they keep their options open and then develop a strategy.

Who you become as an investor is defined by your goals and probably is unlike any of the investors I have discussed. Therefore, finding a fundamental strategy can be difficult. Let's say that your strategy is long term—many years of consistent income—then your fundamental analysis would be different from that of someone who has a one-year goal. But then again, you may be diversified in your strategy, with many goals, something I will discuss in Part IV.

Now that you know the purpose of fundamental data, you must create a fundamental strategy that matches your personal goals. You want to simplify the process and use a specific collection of data to get you moving in the right direction. This step should be taken before you assess a stock's position. This step allows you to first find potential companies based on measurable data, which is what I have discussed throughout this entire chapter, by identifying what's most important for certain goals. Therefore, focus on five key fundamental metrics that best suit your goals as an investor. To better explain this, let's look at the first areas of importance for me as an investor.

This excludes all stock-related valuation metrics and comes strictly from the income statement, balance sheet, and cash flow.

- **Revenue growth.** As a value investor, I want to know that the stock isn't cheap because the business is losing sales. Therefore, I always search for a company with year-over-year revenue growth
- **Earnings growth.** The bottom line is the single most important metric to the valuation of a company and how it's perceived in the market. Therefore, I want to make sure that the bottom line is growing, which should result in positive stock performance, all things considered.
- **Profit margin.** The profit margin reflects efficiency, and I want to know that my investment is growing earnings faster than revenue, therefore becoming more efficient.
- **Debt to assets.** As an investor, I want to know that my investment's assets aren't all debt. A high debt-to-assets ratio can hurt a company in times of distress, and because I am investing in a flat market that is full of uncertainty, I want my investments to be well positioned with a strong balance sheet.
- **Operational cash flow.** Knowing where the money comes from is vital. Is your company returning its income from financing and investing? Or does it come from the day-to-day operations of the company? I want to know that my investment is earning its cash from the operation of its business.

UNMEASURED FUNDAMENTALS

One of the more important areas of concern for a long-term investor is the unmeasured fundamentals. These unmeasured areas have a great deal of importance to long-term investors because they have the potential to move the stock and must be considered in addition to basic fundamental knowledge.

Thus far I have discussed a number of fundamental measures in stock metrics and how to use them to make better investment decisions based on your goals. However, it is extremely important to identify and understand unmeasured fundamentals because they can have a major impact on the performance of a stock. These fundamentals will be easier to understand by breaking them into three subtopics.

Employment Trends

You can actually find information for most companies regarding employment, but it's difficult to measure the happiness and benefits of employees. Obviously, the number of employees who make a career out of working at McDonald's is relatively small, but I do think that the average number of years an employee works at a particular company and the number of executives who have worked their way up do matter in a company regardless of whether it is McDonald's or Ford Motor Company. You must take into consideration that an executive's job is to increase the price of a stock throughout her tenure. Several companies have been known to low-ball their employee salaries and cut benefits in order to achieve fundamental milestones that could affect the stock.

When it comes to employment, the only measure that I weigh heavily is whether the company is hiring or firing. When discussing the income statement, I explained that there are several ways that a company can manipulate its results to post stronger earnings. One way a company may increase its earnings is by laying off a large number of employees while still being profitable and hitting financial goals. This is a red flag to me as an investor.

Whether or not a company is hiring is not necessarily important, but I don't want to see a company firing its employees just to hit earning expectations. I agree with the idea of having the correct number of employees to operate with efficiency, but I do find it worrisome when a company will lay off a large number of employees yet posts hundreds of millions in net income. I think that if you are an investor seeking a long-term investment, it makes more sense to buy stock in a company that can manage to grow without having to lay off employees. When margins increase and income rises but employment has been cut, it really doesn't reflect the effectiveness of management. You are instead left wondering why the company laid off hard-working employees. As an investor, I want my returns to be as large as possible, but not at the cost of people losing their jobs. I would much rather find equally good companies that operate with employees in mind because hard work and good talent equal a successful business that will ultimately grow.

Relationships

Have you ever wondered how Kroger keeps all its stores stocked? Or where Walmart finds its diversified collection of products and services? There are countless moving parts to a large, publically traded company. It's almost like a cascade of dominos, where every domino has to fall smoothly in order for it to be a fully executed "domino effect." If one domino misses its target, the pattern is disrupted and cannot be completed. It's the same with large companies. If any of the truckers decided not to transport goods, then some stores would not be stocked with certain products. The same would apply if a supplier's crop were destroyed by a natural disaster. It could be devastating for a company's revenue, a company that was depending on the supplier's goods. This scenario also could result in a loss of business.

In order for a company to execute perfectly, all its dominos must be in line. As consumers, it is our job to seek and buy the company's product. We don't worry about the chain of events that caused the product to arrive at its destination; we are only concerned with the fact that it is available when we want it. Therefore, an ineffective business model ultimately can lead to a company's deterioration. Regardless of the industry, all companies rely on business relationships to succeed.

A company's relationships may be hard to identify, but they are always worth researching. We can narrow "relationships" into three separate categories: vendors, suppliers, and customers. It would be impossible for you to know every single vendor, supplier, or customer. What is important is knowing that your potential investment has relationships that are solid and can stand the test of time, especially if you are investing for longer than one year. I don't consider this to be the most important measure that should consume your research, but before buying shares in a company, you should always ask yourself if the company's relationships are secure.

Executive Changes

One of the biggest drivers of a stock is the company's changes within management. The management (or executives) will determine the business model and growth strategy and make the decisions that impact day-to-day operations. The right CEO can turn a small-cap company into a billion-dollar company, but the wrong CEO can bring a Fortune 500 company to its knees. Therefore, you need to know all changes in executives and the achievements or failures of the executive team.

The best example of an executive change affecting a stock is with XPO Logistics. This is a company that I own as one of my larger holdings and have followed since June 2011. I didn't begin watching the stock because of its great track record, nor did I buy it because I liked its previous growth strategy. I bought it because of a change at the executive level.

In June 2011, Bradley Jacobs announced that he was investing $150 million into the small company and would be taking over the board as the acting CEO. I immediately bought shares in the company and continued to buy on the dips throughout the following year. Why did I buy shares in this company, and decide to make it one of my largest holdings over a year's time? The answer is Bradley Jacobs. Bradley Jacobs is one of the more successful entrepreneurs that you've most likely never heard of. Jacobs had successfully created and built four multi-billion dollar companies from scratch throughout his career, in several different industries. He has done so with a strategy of maintaining a large cash position at the company, and then growing through acquisitions and cold starts, and then growing the acquisitions and cold starts by each having great synergy with the core business. It may seem like a simply strategy, but Jacobs had a proven history of success with this strategy and always seems to time the growth of an industry very well. For example, in February 2011, Jacobs and I spoke and he said to me that "our freight forwarding unit is a $70 million business in a $150 billion industry." This is a good example of how Jacobs has over the years found a large business, enters it, and then grows it.

In the past, Jacobs had started a company and made it a multibillion company within five years. With XPO Logistics, he was getting an established company with minimal debt and $160 million in revenue. Therefore, with the size of the industry and his strategy of building through acquisitions, it seemed like the perfect fit for a long-term investment. Thus far the return has been 100 percent, and it's a stock that I believe will continue to appreciate mainly because of Jacobs and his decision not only to invest but also to control the company as well.

My investment in XPO Logistics is the perfect example of paying close attention to opportunities that may arise from changes in management. It's a metric that is unmeasured but is crucial to the success of any company. Therefore, I suggest knowing the CEO of any prospective company and his or her track record as an executive. It could very well be the difference between massive gains or losses associated with your investment. If you need proof that this strategy is effective, then just watch XPO Logistics over the next three years and see what happens with Jacobs on board.

YOU AS AN INVESTOR

Let's say that you don't consider yourself to be any of the three investors that I discussed. You believe yourself to be a long-term investor, but you like to trade in certain situations. Most likely your exact goals do not match the characteristics of the situational investor, short-term investor, or long-term investor that I have described. The idea behind showing you the areas of research that are most important to investors, based on strategy, is to help you to simplify the research process.

When you decide to take control of your own finances, there is no doubt that you have weighed the pros and cons and feel as though your decision has been thoroughly evaluated. It is, after all, a very stressful time that can be filled with anxiety and uncertainty. My goal is to make this transition as simple as possible and to simplify the process of investing to the best of my ability. However, the "most important" areas that I have discussed may be irrelevant to you. You will most likely develop your own process of research and focus on metrics that are the most important for your own goals. It is imperative to research and know the meaning behind each metric, but there is no reason to make it any more difficult than necessary because finding a fundamentally strong company is only half the battle.

Warren Buffett said on several occasions that if a company performs well, its stock will usually follow. Because this statement is true, it is of the utmost importance to be able to identify a company that is performing well. It's equally important to be able to identify and capitalize on value when it presents itself in the market. Hopefully, you have learned the fundamental section like the back of your hand, and you know what to look for while searching for a fundamentally strong company. Now it's time to take a look at the psychological aspects of the market. This will help you to identify buying points while eliminating emotion, which will help you to better understand how a market can act without a given reason.

PART III

CHAPTER 9

Behavioral Selling

Everyone has the brainpower to make money in stocks.
Not everyone has the stomach. If you are susceptible to
selling everything in a panic, you ought to avoid stocks
and mutual funds altogether.

—PETER LYNCH

WHAT MOVES A STOCK?

Before you can use the tendencies and reactions of the market to
your benefit, you must understand the basics of behavioral finance.
My primary rule for success in the market is to keep things as simple
as possible. When a stock is volatile and moves either up or down,
it's because there are more traders playing one way.

Over the years, I have been very surprised to learn just how
many people don't understand what drives a stock higher or lower.
This is probably the most basic of information. A stock is driven
higher or lower by supply and demand. When you buy a stock,
someone else is selling it to you. Assuming that there are equal numbers of buyers and sellers, the price of the stock remains the same.

However, a price trades higher when there are more buyers than sellers and trades lower when more people are trying to sell shares.

Let's say that you bought shares of Intel for $25, and the stock is trading at $24 two weeks later. There are a number of reasons the stock may be trading lower. The company may have announced lower than expected earnings, or the market as a whole may have traded lower on weak economic data. Either way, the stock traded lower than the price you paid to acquire it. The reason that Intel fell by $1 is that there were more people selling the stock than were willing to buy it. Also, because of market conditions or whatever factor caused the stock to fall, investors were not willing to buy shares for $25. Therefore, with fewer buyers than sellers, the price of the stock will decline until there is a balance of buyers and sellers or until the price of the stock reaches a level both investors and market makers believe the stock is worth.

WHY ARE THEY SELLING AND IS IT AN OPPORTUNITY?

The reasons people sell their shares of stock are seemingly limitless. They may have decided to end a 20-year investment, or they may need cash or have to pay their child's tuition. People sell for a variety of reasons. The question you have to ask yourself is whether the sell is warranted. As a value investor, it's your goal to buy undervalued stocks. The only way to buy undervalued stocks is to buy them below their worth, which is usually on the downside or when there are significantly more sellers than buyers. Therefore, you must determine the reasons that the market is selling. Is it because of a down market, or is it because the company lowered its earning guidance by a significant margin? If you can correctly acquire stocks that are falling for the wrong reasons, most likely you will be able to return very large profits over an extended period of time.

As a value investor, I like to think that every stock I purchase is bought with value in mind. I always try to make rational decisions and avoid becoming excited because I know that sudden surges in emotion can lead to mistakes. I feel that understanding why a stock falls may be the most important aspect of being a good value investor. The price you pay for a stock will determine your return. For example, if you have $10,000 and buy a stock at $20 and it rises to $25, then you are going to have solid gains. But if you are patient and wait for the stock to fall even lower, you may be able to buy it at $15. Then your return will be much larger. The problem with this strategy is that sometimes the stock will not fall to a lower level, and then you miss out on possible gains. This fact is one of the leading reasons that people make hasty decisions and buy a stock too high. They may lose sight of their long-term goal, get caught in the moment, and then decide to buy.

The argument for not waiting to buy does hold some ground because we don't know for certain which direction a stock will trend over a period of several months. My theory is that there are way too many great stocks in the market to buy one at face value. I simply refuse to buy a stock unless it has fallen or is inappropriately valued. It doesn't necessarily have to be trading at all-time lows, but it does need to present a price that is hard to justify.

After reading this book, you may think that it is the most worthless collection of words ever published, and if so, that's okay. However, there are certain points that I want you to remember, and hopefully, reading this book can change or at least open your mind to new perspectives because learning when to buy and sell is very important. It ultimately determines whether you gain or lose. With that being said, you must know that perception on Wall Street changes according to price. If you can understand this fact, you will be long on your way to thinking and acting as a value investor who returns profits. Let me explain.

When a stock is trading higher, all information is positive, but when it trades lower, all information is negative. It's really that simple. Investors are a product of the moment and are so afraid of losing a dollar that they never stop to look and analyze their own behavior. Even the most intelligent professional on Wall Street is incapable of controlling the emotions driven by price and performance. When the market is trading lower, you will hear people say that it's because there are significant weaknesses all over the globe; therefore, investors are reacting to a troublesome airline industry (for example). But when the market is trading higher, everything is great in the economy. Those same people who were negative now believe that it's time to buy, and the change of opinions may only be days apart.

This behavior has always seemed a little backward to me because it makes more sense that you would want to buy when the market is trading lower and sell when it is trading higher so that you get the best bang for your buck. Because we constantly search for answers and are blinded by the moment, some of us are almost incapable of buying when the stock or market trades lower, even though we understand the reasons that it would be most beneficial to buy a security at its lowest price.

Such an example can be seen in the financial industry with stocks such as Citigroup, Bank of America, Wells Fargo, and Goldman Sachs. The most recent example of our change in perspective occurred in 2011, when the market pulled back in the final six months led by the financials and the automotive industry. It's interesting that it was these two industries that traded substantially lower because the market feared a potential default in several European countries. These were the industries most affected during the recession, and when faced with the fear of another recession in 2011, regardless of whether it was a European recession, the markets reacted and sold stocks in these two industries. I think that this is a perfect example of cause and effect from the negative reinforcement created during the financial crisis. In 2011, the same fear was sparked, but there were few similarities in the state of the economy. The auto industry was perhaps the strongest in the market during 2011, so why would it trade so low during the sell-off? The large money center banks did have a connection to Europe, so some of the market's losses were appropriate. However, stocks in the automotive and even regional banking industry traded lower with minimal justification as to why.

My only explanation is that investors were simply reacting to selling pressure and then selling what they believed were the most vulnerable industries because of the recession. How else could you explain the performance of regional banks such as Huntington Bancshares during the months of July and August when the market lost so much of its value? The stock lost 30 percent of its value, but the company has very few, if any, ties to Europe because of it being such a small regional banking company. Therefore, the loss was not valid based on the events that were pushing the stock lower. As a result, the stock presented value to investors who were able to see that Huntington's loss had no connection to the events that were pushing the market lower. Those who purchased at the low levels in August 2011 enjoyed a very nice 50 percent return over the following six months as the opinions regarding the company went from negative to positive and the price of the stock traded higher.

The difference between 2009 and 2011 is that the financial crisis of 2009 was driven by very real events, and in 2011 it was driven by speculation and a fear that history would repeat itself. The reason that I think 2011 is such a good example of strong selling creating opportunity is because it was obvious that the selling was unwarranted. In 2009, corporate earnings were falling, credit and/ or financing just about collapsed, and the housing market tanked completely. In 2011, corporate earnings were rising, unemployment was stalled but still had shown progress, and there were no other noticeable reasons for these banking stocks to be trading with such devastating loss. I am not saying that the industry shouldn't have lost some of its worth, but the loss should have been nowhere near what it was during the final six months of 2011.

In the case of the auto industry, both General Motors and Ford were posting incredible monthly sale gains and pushing units at a remarkable rate. In fact, the auto industry probably was the strongest industry in the market. Yet both stocks dropped 40 percent in just a few short months with very little news pertaining to either company. In fact, the only news from either company was that monthly sales were increasing by high single and low double digits, which is an encouraging development that indicates strength in an industry.

The question you must ask yourself when a stock falls is: Why is the stock falling? Is it because of a bankruptcy or some other key development that directly affects future earnings? Or is it a reaction caused by fear or a domino effect that cannot be explained. When a stock does fall, you have to determine whether or not the degree of loss is appropriate. This can all be a little tricky because as you are trying to determine whether or not the fall is fundamentally or emotionally caused, the perception on Wall Street will be changing. Remember, we as humans must seek answers and make things more difficult than they are. Therefore, we cannot settle for the simple fact that a stock may have fallen for no logical reason, and when it does happen, sometimes we can't identify it. With Bank of America, there were analysts, money managers, and other professionals saying to sell at $6 when it was obvious that the stock was ridiculously cheap. Although these people are smart and very well educated, they just got caught in the same emotional roller coaster that is the stock market.

SPRINT: PERCEPTION AND PRICE RELATIONSHIP

One of my favorite stocks is Sprint Nextel (ticker symbol S). I don't like the stock because I think it is the greatest company in the world but rather because I believe that it is valued particularly low. My opinion regarding this company has gone from two completely different extremes in a period of less than one year. Take a look at a direct quote I published in an article entitled, "The Future of Communication Stocks," on August 12, 2011, in regard to Sprint Nextel:

> The company has demonstrated a failure to improve financially by posting more loss each year since 2008. Sprint has seen assets decrease over the last four years, yet keeps long-term debt in the same range. I believe the company's operations revolve around the idea of removing assets to keep debt from increasing to cover the true effect of a company that cannot produce a profit. This concept or strategy may work for a while but eventually will cost the company. With AT&T and Verizon expanding operations and Sprint seeing no income from Apple's success, I believe the

stock will fall further. After looking over the income statements
and balance sheet, I do not see how the company can create
value that exceeds the market cap.

During the first half of 2011, Sprint was trading with gains and
reached a price over $6 per share. Much like the auto and financial
industries, the stock then fell in the later months of 2011. As you
can see from my quote, I was definitely not bullish on the company.
It had way too much debt and was still far from reaching any level
of profitability. Yet the market felt that it was worth a price of more
than $5 per share or a $15 billion in market capitalization. In fact,
when the stock was $4.50, two respective firms, Kaufman Brothers
and Argus, both upgraded the stock.

Before we go any further, allow me to explain the relevance of
an analyst upgrading or downgrading a stock's performance. When
an analyst upgrades or downgrades a stock, the market reacts and
either buys or sells because investors believe enough due diligence
has been done to assume that the analyst will be close in his price or
performance prediction. Some analysts have a tremendous amount of
resources and often specialize in one particular sector or industry of
the market, which gives them even more credibility. Therefore, when
one of these highly regarded individuals speaks, everyone listens.

A good analyst can provide reason in times of madness. He can
look at only the facts and then release an educated opinion based on
the facts, research, and other materials used to determine a rating.
Now with Sprint, two fairly respected analysts upgraded the stock
to $4.50, but six months later following the sell-off in the market in
2011, Sprint was trading at about $2.50. These same firms down-
graded the stock and changed their opinion. This was due in part
to the stock's performance against the market and in part to the
expectations of the company.

My guidance and outlook for Sprint changed from pessimistic
to optimistic about the same time that the two analysts downgraded
the stock. It still had all the same problems that I mentioned in my
published article, but at $2.50, I felt that it was a much better bargain

or value. However, the change of opinion among analysts shows the mind-set on Wall Street. When a stock is trading higher, even the brightest of the bright are optimistic. Once it trades lower, everyone becomes negative.

As I said, Sprint still had the same problems at $4.50 as it did at $2.50; it still had too much debt, falling subscribers, network issues, and too many worthless locations that produced very little in revenue. The only difference was the price of the stock. Oh, and there was one other small difference for the company—and that was the iPhone! The iPhone is the most sought-after device in the world, and I believe that it has the ability to change the outlook for Sprint and save the company. After just two quarters, the company has increased revenue and subscribers, which were the two areas that had been falling. Yet people are still pessimistic and believe that with increased revenue and subscribers, the company is worth 40 percent less than it was one year ago. Today, Sprint is trading at $2.29, and I promise that by the time this book is published, the stock will be trading at least 75 percent higher. I don't think it takes a rocket scientist to see that it's undervalued, just a little common sense to realize that improving fundamentals equal a better company and a stock that is sure to follow.

THE MOST IMPORTANT POINT TO REMEMBER ABOUT MARKET PSYCHOLOGY

Hopefully, my examples of Huntington Bancshares and Sprint provided some insight into the importance of price. The price of a stock is very crucial to understanding the behavior of the market because the price of a stock is the price that investors are willing to pay to own a piece of the company. The price isn't always going to be correct and will not always make sense, but then again, very few things in life are always black and white and can be labeled as correct or logical. Therefore, you must use your best judgment to identify value and determine whether or not value is present in a market that is very opinionated.

Before I became a full-time investor, I worked for the state of Kentucky as a counselor for the Department of Corrections. My job was to counsel men who had been in and out of the prison system and help them to adjust to life outside prison and prepare for life in a crime-free setting. It was probably the most rewarding job I ever had because it was always great to meet someone who really wanted to change and who would take all the necessary steps to succeed. However, it was also very frustrating because sometimes I would work with people who had all the potential to do something great with their lives but just couldn't avoid drugs or proved incapable of making better decisions.

I often would see the same people circulating through the system every year, and it was always sad to know that their lives were wasted and that they most likely would spend the majority of their adult lives in prison for a multitude of crimes. I remember one class in particular where I finally lost it and began going through all the reasons to quit using drugs and stop robbing grocery stores. I talked with my students about how they would never get to fully experience children or watch them grow. I also tried to get them to realize that criminal activity has a tendency of getting passed from generation to generation; and that their actions could and most likely would be passed on to their children. I would also discuss facts and data showing the amount of income that is lost over a lifetime by being incarcerated, and that their decisions could now impact their livelihood; and the livelihood of their children. Regardless of this logic, which would make perfectly good sense to you and me, it did not affect these particular people. To some, I might as well have been teaching calculus because their concept of normal and my idea of normal were not particularly aligned.

Regardless of how many psychology classes you take in college or how many degrees you earn, I don't think there is anyone who could fully comprehend the thought process of a career criminal or someone who has lived a life of crime and refuses to change. The only thing that allowed me to keep my sanity was a constant reminder that what's logical to me just seems illogical to them. I used to tell myself this over and over throughout the day. I have since carried it with me through life into marriage, work, and dealing with family and in-laws. Anytime someone has a different perspective or opinion or action that is different from mine, I remind myself of a very simple truth that I have carried with me and that also has allowed me to understand the market in a much more efficient manner.

Over the years, there have been several great books that detail mass behavior and financial tendencies. The truth is, however, that we can't say or predict with 100 percent certainty how a group of people will react to a situation. We are a collection of people with different backgrounds, social lives, morals, religions, ethics, and so on who all come together as one. This mixture combines to create market insanity and actions that may appear logical to me but illogical to someone else or that are irrational to me but rational to someone else.

If I spend too much time talking about Sprint and its valuation, I may become somewhat defensive or even angry. I may want people to view it with the same level of value as I do. This is so because of the way I have been trained to identify value, which is nothing more than my personality tendencies that all come together in the way that I perform research. We all see something different when we look at art or at clouds in the sky. Our every action is a reaction of a previous experience that caused us to become methodical. As an investor, if you can understand and realize these tendencies or patterns caused by experiences, you can profit by remaining calm in a market that is fueled by emotion. Basically, this involves understanding your strengths and weaknesses so that you can remain calm and not allow your emotions to make decisions in an overly emotional market.

As you progress in this book, I am going to talk in much more detail about emotions and reactions that fuel the market. I can't tell you exactly when to buy or when to sell because if there were such a formula, it would mean that the market is logical, and that would mean that logic has the same meaning to all people. The market is not logical. In fact, it's the most illogical platform you will ever encounter. It's this lack of logic you are trying to find that is sometimes hidden from the naked eye because of our own tendencies. In the end, it's easy to look back on the performance of Huntington and see value in its late 2011 price. The trick is knowing that the value is present before it starts to rise and being able to see it when everyone else is telling you that it doesn't exist. With that being said, ask yourself a very simple question if you ever find yourself considering a stock that is being sold: Why is it being sold? Can you logically explain why it is being sold, or can anyone else logically explain why they are selling? Does it make sense, like a career criminal who refuses to better his life? What is the rationale behind the selling? Most likely you will find that selling pressure is almost never driven by any sense of logic or a rational thought process but rather by panic and fear. Therefore, as you progress into this section on market psychology, I will explain why and how panic is your best friend.

CHAPTER 10

Panic Is Your Best Friend

Be fearful when others are greedy and greedy only when
others are fearful.

—WARREN BUFFETT

The process of understanding market behavior may seem a bit overwhelming, but in reality, it's not that bad when you know how to
simplify it. You keep the basic information simple and don't make
the more difficult aspect any harder than it has to be. Market tendencies and why people react a certain way with their finances has
been studied for years. In psychology, we can predict and understand behavior based on childhood, social class, family size, and so
on, but in the market, such an analysis involves much more than
understanding the simple actions of an individual person. You are
trying to understand the tendencies of a collection of people who all
possess different goals and objectives.

Honestly, it would be almost impossible to develop a somewhat
reasonable theory that explains the totality of market behavior. You
can't do it because the market is such a large collection of people who
all have different behaviors. Since all the factors used when discuss-

ing financial behavior are based on the perception of an individual person or even a collection of people who are somehow classified together, it would be impossible to draw a reasonable and consistent conclusion about market behavior. There are just too many individual personalities with different spending tendencies and goals. Therefore, you must search for the common denominators and/or emotions that everyone in the market or at least a vast majority may share regardless of individual goals or preferences.

As value investors, there are certain psychological indicators that we seek that may indicate value. The best are fear and panic because they are widespread; they are both contagious and steal the rationale from logically thinking people.

You may wonder why fear and panic are so important to the success of a value investor, so allow me to explain. Let me start by saying that there are thousands of publically traded companies that all have individual investors. In Chapter 17, I explained how there is no-one-size-fits all investment strategy. The primary goal is to return gains. If your fundamental analysis is different from mine, and we purchase two completely different companies that both return gains of 10 percent, then it doesn't really matter whose strategy for choosing stocks is better—the end result is the same, and everything else is just a matter of opinion. The point to remember is that investing is proud. At any given moment, you can turn to CNBC and hear two or three equally intelligent people discuss completely different opinions on the same company. This doesn't necessarily mean that one is right and the other is wrong, but it is proof of just how wide the road to success can be in the market. Yet, because there are so many different and effective ways to succeed and so many publically traded companies, this means that when you decide on a particular stock from a pool of thousands, you have an immediate emotional attachment to that security.

It may sound weird to identify an investment as an emotional attachment, but the characteristics are very similar to those in a relationship. When you decide on an investment or a stock to purchase, there must be some reason or factor that leads you to believe that it is better than all the rest. Emotions and beliefs such as this can be very strong and also can blind you to making rational decisions. It is important to look at stocks without bias because this attachment starts the process of emotion, which can lead to bad decisions that cause responses such as panic or fear when your hypothesis is proven to be incorrect.

PANIC AND FEAR

For now, I will abandon the relationship discussion and turn my attention to the topic of panic and fear. The difference between panic and fear is actually quite simple: Fear is an emotion, and panic is an action. If you look back at the last six months of 2011, you will see a perfect example of fear that turned to panic.

The events that played out during the final six months of 2011 were truly the best example of the panic/fear relationship that I can remember. During this time, the economy experienced financial problems caused by failed debt negotiations, but in actuality, the problems were first sparked by the second bailout of Greece. The second bailout marked the first day of a four-week period during which the Dow Jones Industrial Average lost nearly 2,000 points. The reason it was so significant is because it proved that Greece was still incapable of paying off its debt. This forced investors and analysts to take a look at the state of Europe as a whole, and they realized that its economy was in far worse shape than the economy of just one country.

Around the same time that Greece was being bailed out, investors were selling bonds of European countries that also were indebted. In so doing, they were trying to avoid a domino effect of financial hardship in Europe that included Italian and Spanish bonds. This was important because it symbolized panic that other countries would experience the same fate and caused fear among American investors that the financial troubles could reach us or slow down growth because the United States is so closely connected to Europe and other economies.

The second bailout in Greece, along with the selling of European bonds, may have started the sell-off in the U.S. market, but it was definitely the events that followed that pushed the U.S. market to the nearly 2,000 point loss in just under four weeks. I think that just about everyone can remember the series of meetings or debates that occurred at the end of July when politicians had until August 2 to trim debt from our $14 trillion deficit. The deficit in the United States was very scary to investors because they were seeing the devastation in Europe unfold because of too much debt. Our politicians could not agree on any cuts during several days of negotiations as the president missed promised deadlines, and it became a political war between Democrats and Republicans, who were pointing the blame at each other on a daily basis.

The debate on how to cut the nation's mountain of debt was as great an indicator of a partisan divide as we have seen in many years. The fear was that if an agreement was not reached, it could lead to a government shutdown and/or a downgrade of the U.S credit rating. These fears were made a reality on August 5 when Standard & Poor's downgraded the U.S. credit rating for the first time in history. By this time, fear of our debt affecting the system had already turned to widespread panic. More than $3 trillion dollars disappeared from the market during the first week of August as investors anticipated the downgraded rating. The Federal Reserve had done all it could by keeping interest rates low, but real fear still existed that a lower credit rating ultimately could mean higher interest rates for mortgages, loans, and even college tuition.

The final six months of 2011 were pure panic created by a chain of events over a period of several months. We had already seen the financial distress in Europe, and now our nation's debt was far from reaching a resolution. However, I don't think that many people believed that we could actually have our credit downgraded. But as a result of the fear already present, we assumed the worst of what could result from a downgrade.

WHY SELL?

Throughout 2011, we were somewhat fearful that Europe's financial problems could affect U.S. corporate earnings. Therefore, the markets remained on edge and never really welcomed strong corporate earnings. Even during the sell-off in the final six months of 2011, corporate earnings were very strong, but we wouldn't allow ourselves to get too excited. The truth is that when we are dealing with investments and money, we are always somewhat fearful. The fear is always present. It just takes something to turn that fear into panic. Usually it's a result of selling pressure, and we sell without understanding the reason why we are selling.

Fear exists only because we don't want to lose our money. For investors, a loss isn't a loss until the stock is sold, and once the loss is realized, we have a tendency to become desperate in an attempt to "win back" our loss. Given the state of the "new era" of investing, we are seeing investors holding less and buying more frequently.

The first 10 years of the millennium were a flat decade that most likely affected anyone who invested during that time. If you were using a money manager, you owned Internet companies during the dot-com bubble and were invested into the financial system during the recession. It's not bad that you may have owned these stocks as they fell because they were overvalued as a result of many investors believing that they were worth their valuations. There were many people who got hurt during this time (remember the getting burnt analogy), and people simply couldn't afford to lose their money.

There are some people who held the money center banks during the recession and owned companies such as Cisco that looked very strong during the dot-com era. These people still may be recovering. Therefore, it makes sense that people would sell and push stocks ridiculously low and lose their ability to comprehend value in fear of losing more money. Yet it's these experiences, such as being exposed during the recession and owning momentum stocks during the dot-com era, that have now caused us to invest with such fear.

Investors are now incapable of looking months ahead because they are so worried about what's going to happen tomorrow. As a result, there are fewer long-term investors and more active traders who usually return losses, thanks to a very natural release of endorphins that tells them to buy when the market trades higher.

Our actions are a result of our environment. When it comes to the market, most people who have been buying stocks for the last decade are easily discouraged by any sign of loss regardless of what's causing the loss because of past bad experience. As a result, there are many who don't have the patience to buy on the dips or hold a stock for any extended period of time to allow it to appreciate. This causes even more frustration and panic when potential gains are lost. At this point, it's a sick cycle of continuous loss and a desperate attempt to get back to even as quickly as possible that causes investors to lose their perception of logic.

In today's market, retail investors feel as though they must be active to profit. There are days when the Dow Jones will trade in a 200-point range, meaning that decent gains can be wiped away for large loss in a matter of hours. It's a devastating reality to see gains diminish or see a loss increase. I know how it feels, and it can be devastating. When you've done your homework and believe that you have bought a good stock that will rise, it can be disconcerting to watch the stock drop lower for reasons that you can't understand. Sometimes you can't understand why a stock is trading lower because there are no logical reasons, yet you continue to fall in the same trap and sell yourself short to avoid an immediate loss.

The first step to becoming a good value investor who returns market-leading gains is to eliminate emotion. The only way to eliminate emotion is to limit your activity. In Chapter 12, I will explain how you can be active yet passive and still return the best gains by completely eliminating all emotions from a buy and a sell. The most important point at this particular moment is to understand that people sometimes sell without knowing why just to avoid a loss and that this action (panic) is what can ultimately return gains once you know how to control it and identify it in the actions of others.

BUY LOW, SELL HIGH

The most important factor to returning large gains in the market is to know when to buy a stock. The goal is to buy low and sell high. As I have explained, though, this is a very difficult action for many investors. I can't count how many times someone has asked me how I know when it is a good time to buy a particular stock, as if there is some kind of price that will return immediate gains.

Unfortunately, the market is constantly evolving, and this is so because the companies that make up the market are constantly changing. Some companies' earnings, spending, goals, products, and even management are constantly changing. The range of a stock can always change as well. Hopefully, if you've done your homework and found a company with strong fundamental growth, then the future trend of the stock should be higher. Yet, because of illogical trends in the market and our tendency to overreact to any news, stocks that should trend higher often trade lower.

Take a look at Figure 10.1 and you will see a stock that reflects the flat decade of the 2000s. You also will see how indecisive investors have been when buying and selling this stock. Finally, you will

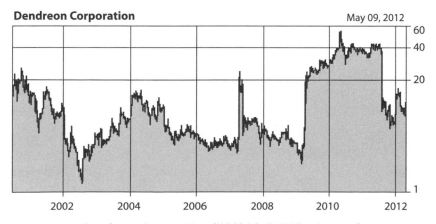

Figure 10.1   **Dendreon Corporation (NASDAQ: DNDN) price performance over a 10-year period prior to May 9, 2012.**

see how the price paid to purchase a stock is the ultimate provider of either gains or losses. The stock we're looking at is in the company Dendreon, which is a very controversial company that has been in the spotlight since it became a public company because of its cancer drug Provenge. The stock has always traded with an incredible amount of volatility because investors in this stock have returned either enormous gains or devastating losses.

Right now I want you to study the chart and count how many times the stock trades significantly higher with strong trends and look for peaks both at the top and at the bottom. Most likely you see three different periods where the stock trades with unusual volatility, but if you were to break this chart into a yearly chart for the last 11 years, you would notice that Dendreon actually has traded with extreme periods of volatility on about 30 occasions. You can't see it because the data on the chart are measures of weekly performance.

There are two key points that I want you to remember about the price paid for a stock. Unexplainable trends higher are a trap, and extended periods of loss may indicate a good buy. Remember, when a stock is trading higher, the media, investors, the company, and the newspapers are all excited, but when the stock trades lower, everyone is negative. The key is to practice using the tools I have discussed, such as remaining calm and asking yourself why did the stock fall and was the loss worth the event that caused it to fall. In some cases, there aren't any catalysts from the company that cause the stock to fall; it's just a result of market activity. In other cases, it may be value. However, there is one more area that must be explained. If you simply buy when a stock starts to trade lower, then you might still lose.

If you bought Dendreon (ticker symbol DNDN) in 2000 at $14, in May of 2012 you would have returned a very large loss. You even may argue that you bought the stock as it was trading lower in the year 2000. It reached a high over $20 and then traded lower, but you still returned a loss. This is where your ability to identify value comes into play.

In 2000, you should have known that this developmental company without revenue was not worth a $3 billion valuation, especially considering the time it would take for the company to be awarded Food and Drug Administration approval for its new drug. The high valuations and distinction of value in biotechnology are one of the hardest areas to judge, but I will discuss biotechnology later. For now, let's continue our focus on the valuation and price performance of Dendreon.

Thus, if you bought Dendreon in 2000 at $14, you most likely bought the stock as it was trading lower. However, if you were holding in May 2012, then you would have returned a loss. The key to buying low has nothing to do with price; it's all about value, and there is a big difference between something cheap and something valuable. You must understand fundamental growth and how to identify a healthy, fast-growing company or else your ability to understand the psychology of the market is irrelevant.

The final factor to consider when buying low and selling high is that periods of volatility are always going to produce extreme price fluctuations that result in stocks being too high or too low. A stock almost always falls lower than it should and rises higher than it should during periods of extreme volatility. When a stock is trading in either a downtrend or an uptrend, there always comes a point when it bottoms out or reaches its peak and then reverses.

A stock is carried by momentum, and investors are always trying to ride a trend higher. Therefore, once a trend is noticed, it causes a domino effect of people buying to try to capitalize on gains. It's very similar to when investors sell a stock to avoid loss or just because it's trading lower. The same is true for when it trades higher. The only difference is that when a stock trades higher, everyone is positive; and when it trades lower, we are all negative. As a result, we often get caught holding longer than we should or buy a stock too high because of its uptrend. After all, we don't want to miss out on the opportunity to buy a stock trading higher. However, to be safe, you should never buy when the stock is trading higher by large margins. There are hundreds of good companies in the market, and there is not one that is too good to buy for any price not considered "flea-market value." Just be patient; your goal is to buy at the bottom, not at the top.

When a stock has strong selling pressure and falls for several days or months, it is your job to determine the reason for the loss. This is one of the first steps when buying a value stock. If the stock is trading lower as a result of market conditions but is still posting good corporate earnings and hasn't given any indications that any trouble awaits, then it may be a good time to buy the stock after its fall. A good example is General Motors during the sell-off in 2011. From July to December, the stock went from $31 to $19 before finally reversing and trading back to nearly $30 in February of 2012. General Motors and Ford were falling with authority during the final six months of 2011, and there was no real catalyst from either company. There were periods when both companies would make an announcement that was less than optimistic, but there was nothing to entice such strong selling in either stock. In fact, both companies were among the few strengths of the economy. Both were posting very impressive monthly sales numbers and giving guidance to suggest significant growth, including Ford's 50 percent sales growth forecast by 2015.

With both Ford and General Motors trading lower in 2011, it would have been a good time for investors to take advantage of the value. Both companies had very strong fundamentals (which are the first area of research) and were trading with very attractive metrics, such as price/earnings (P/E) ratios below 5, and they were falling owing to speculation not facts. Therefore, the ability to think rationally and realize that both stocks were trading lower because of market conditions and that both would reverse at some point in the near future would have returned very healthy gains. This "ability" shouldn't have been difficult, considering the guidance and sales growth from both companies.

The idea of buying when a stock trades to new lows or is in a strong downtrend doesn't always return gains. The key to ensuring that it will return gains is to identify value, which is the ability to identify fundamentally strong companies that are growing. You want to make sure that the company was fairly valued before it began to fall and had healthy stock metrics, as I discussed in Chapters 7 and 8. You need to understand that if a stock trades in an uptrend for several years, it can easily lose 20 to 30 percent of its gains with one bad earnings report if the stock's performance was far better than its earnings growth during the same period. You need to determine whether one bad earnings report was worth the reaction that it caused. If the stock traded with a five-year return of 500 percent and traded with a P/E ratio multiple of 70, then a 30 percent loss may very well be appropriate because the market was pricing the stock with the idea that its earnings would be great. However, if the stock posts the same loss and barely missed earnings expectations and trades with a P/E ratio of only 10, then it could be presenting value.

The point is that you want to avoid stocks that trade in uptrends that last several consecutive years with high stock metrics. These companies are considered momentum stocks with expensive metrics and are priced to always outperform all expectations. When the company misses expectations, it can cause excessive loss. When a company that has high expectations but doesn't meet the expectations, its stock can trade lower by 20 percent, and it does not necessarily mean that you should buy the stock or that value is present. You only want to buy a stock that has healthy trading metrics and falls by an unexplained margin for reasons that don't make sense. The last thing you want is to buy a stock at the top of its peak because when it reverses, the loss will always be significant. However, if you buy a stock with strong fundamentals and healthy trading metrics at the bottom of its downward "peak," then you are sure to return very large gains. The key is not buying a momentum stock that was destined to fall or a stock that fell but was trading with metrics that were too high; these losses are often sensible. You want stocks that fall for unexplained reasons when the margin of loss doesn't validate the development that enticed the reaction.

QUESTIONS ABOUT CHAPTER 10

Why are fear and panic the best emotions to identify in the market?

Any emotions are good to identify, but these two are the ones that allow for the most potential upside. You can identify excessive optimism if you plan to short a stock. You want to identify emotions that are contagious, and these emotions are universal in a market that is made up of individuals with unique characteristics. Both fear and panic force people to make stupid decisions and sell to avoid loss, therefore sometimes causing stocks to fall below their worth.

Why do we express fear and panic in the market?

Money is at stake, and we don't want to lose one of the most precious assets in our life. We work hard for our money; therefore, when we realize a loss of our money, it leads us to try to earn it back as quickly as possible.

How can I determine if a stock is priced too high?

You should always compare its price with the company's performance and earnings growth, which is a strategy that I will explain in Chapter 14.

What is a momentum stock?

This is a stock that grows faster than its earnings growth, which is usually characterized by high P/E and price/sales ratios. These companies must continue to outperform all expectations, and if not, they can fall very quickly and with authority. Just look at Netflix.

Is there ever a time when it is good to buy a stock that is trading higher?

Hopefully, you get the opportunity to buy when the stock is trading flat or lower, but sometimes there is nothing wrong with buying a stock that is trading higher. It depends on the valuation. If a stock is valued cheap, such as General Motors, it's okay to buy if you plan to hold for a long time. It all depends on the value of the stock. If a stock trades with a very high valuation compared with its earnings, then you never want to buy it when it's trading higher. If it trades with a very low valuation compared with earnings and is trading higher, then you are still buying at a good price.

If a stock posts a large loss following an earnings report, then how do I know if the loss presents value?

Let's take a look at Chapter 11.

The Earnings Game

Every once in a while, the market does something so stupid it takes your breath away.

—JIM CRAMER

In theory, the market should be driven by fundamentals, but in reality, it is driven by events. What does this mean? It means that market performance and company valuations should be determined by fundamentals, which are corporate earnings. However, the market is event-driven, which means that we often ignore *fundamental* progress and trade according to economic events, rumors, and speculation. This can and does cause fear that leads to panic. As a result, we sell stocks with great fundamentals that should be trading higher.

The good news about a market that is event-driven is that it creates value in stocks. Remember, when a company does well, the stock usually follows. Therefore, you can buy a stock when earnings and guidance are good, but the stock still trades lower for unexplainable reasons. Earnings are what create valuations in the market because stocks are nothing more than a reflection of earnings, and the market is nothing more than a collection of companies that we call stocks.

Every day the market is driven by catalysts such as unemployment data, housing data, and speeches and the economic outlook of politicians and/or analysts. But no other event creates more activity for a particular stock than corporate earnings. When we sell a stock following a market moving catalyst, it's because we believe that the catalyst could affect earnings. Basically, earnings are everything in the market. They are why we buy and sell stocks because we believe earnings will either rise or fall. When there is an announcement or key development within the economy, it causes the market to fall because the market believes that the event could somehow affect earnings.

If the market were a perfectly run machine, earnings would be an easy catalyst to return large gains. However, earnings are based on expectations from the market because most stocks are priced according to future expectations. For example, if a company is expected to post an earnings growth of 20 percent but has a history of exceeding expectations, then it may trade higher before earnings. If it misses expectations, it will most likely trade lower following earnings because the market expected it not only to meet expectations but also to exceed them. It doesn't necessarily matter if earnings are growing because the expectations are the only thing that matters. However, sometimes even if earnings expectations are surpassed, the stock will trade lower. I know it seems confusing at the moment, but let me explain why earnings drive the market and how you can accumulate a substantial amount of value by learning to identify inconsistencies.

I have made substantial money by playing the trends of earnings, and I have witnessed and played every reaction under the sun. There is no other catalyst to better describe the behavior of the market. Some of the reactions following earnings are incredible. When a stock trades lower following a great report, it may be your best opportunity to buy. I have talked about buying low and selling high, and if you can master earnings and knowing how to play the reactions, then your ability to buy low will become much more effective.

In this chapter, I am going to discuss several different reactions following earnings so that you can see firsthand the behavior of the market at its best. I have included several examples that illustrate different ways that you can use the reactions to earnings and buy cheap. Remember, there is no stock that it too good to buy at face value. Earnings can present you with the opportunity to buy a stock far below its worth. Think of it like a garage sale, and as a value investor, you are trying to find the diamond among all the junk.

SODA—EXPECTATIONS CAUSE DIFFERENT RESULTS

Sodastream (ticker symbol SODA) is a controversial company that has grown at a healthy rate for each of the last six years. It's a company that has existed for much longer than we realize, but it hit a growth spurt back in 2010. The company has been controversial because some investors believe that its products are nothing more than a fad. The company creates, markets, and sells home soda makers and has added new retailers to its list of companies that sell its products. Sodastream also has an electric soda maker that will be released before this book is on the shelves that some investors believe could reach restaurants, hotels, and other business establishments. Yet, despite its growth, some investors are still pessimistic about its future and are unwilling to invest in the company.

Right now, SODA is priced at $33 and is a stock that I think is a perfect value investment. The stock is trading at the same price as it was back in 2010 despite $100 million in additional revenue and earnings. The company's earnings have been strong, but the stock is yet to trade with any level of consistent momentum. To better explain this, let's take a look at its performance in 2012 prior to the company's first two earnings reports of the year (Figure 11.1).

In Figure 11.1 you see a three-month range between February 15 and May 15, 2012. This chart is a perfect example of expectations in the market and how they affect a stock. The two periods that are important are the last 15 days of February and the last 15 days of May because these are the two periods before and after the company announced its corporate earnings. You also will notice that both these periods have the highest level of volume, which is reflected

SodaStream International Ltd.   May 15, 2012

Figure 11.1   SodaStream International (NASDAQ: SODA) price performance over a five-year period prior to May 15, 2012.

in the chart below the stock's three-month performance. This is important because it identifies strong movement in the stock.

In the five days prior to SODA announcing earnings in February 2012, the stock traded from $38 to near $48. The gains were more than 25 percent in the days prior to earnings because the market expected SODA to exceed expectations by a large margin. The company had added so many new retailers that investors believe that it would far exceed any and all expectations. Therefore, investors bought shares of the stock before earnings thinking that it would pop after earnings. What they didn't anticipate is that after a 25 percent gain before earnings, the high expectations had already been priced into the stock.

On February 29, SODA traded from $48 to below $41 and then proceeded to fall further to $35 in the days that followed. The reason for the falling price was that the company did not beat expectations or post the earnings that the market expected. The stock had increased to $48 because the market was expecting a massive beat. This means that the stock was then trading with higher metrics, such as a higher price/earnings (P/E) ratio and a higher price/sales ratio. When this happens, the stock becomes more dangerous, and 90 percent of the time, high expectations are already priced into the stock. Therefore, regardless of earnings, the stock will trade lower. Usually, however, it doesn't trade with this level of loss. Because SODA missed expectations when the market was expecting it to blow away expectations, the stock became crushed, and all previous gains were erased.

Now let's fast forward a few months to May. The first thing you should notice is that the trend is completely different. Back in February, the stock traded higher before earnings, but in May, it traded lower before earnings. The reason it traded lower is because the company missed expectations in the previous quarter; therefore, the market expected the company to miss expectations once again. This is how the market—and more specifically, a stock—works. A company's previous earnings often can dictate the direction of its stock for the following three months. It doesn't matter if the company improves its earnings by 20 percent over the previous year. If analysts were expecting the company to improve by 22 percent over the previous year, and the stock traded higher, leading up to the corporate earnings announcement, then its 20 percent progress is irrelevant, and the stock will trade lower or flat until the next time the company releases earnings. This may not make sense, but in some cases 20 percent growth is viewed as negative on Wall Street and causes a stock to fall by a large margin until the company can announce earnings that beat expectations.

In May, the stock fell before earnings, but because it beat expectations, it traded higher following the announcement. Here's the thing: When a stock trades higher for several consecutive years or has one year of very large gains, it is most likely because it has beat expectations for several consecutive quarters. When this happens, analysts haven't yet been able to predict its growth. Sooner or later the analysts will catch up and exceed the company's growth, which causes the stock to drop or to correct. It's the same way with the market except that the overall market is based on economic indicators. We set goals for the economy based on such things as unemployment, and as long as the goals are being met or exceeded, then the market trades higher. As soon as the market doesn't exceed expectations, though, it trades lower. Stocks and the market are nothing more than a chain of events that cause a series of trends, and sometimes you will be able to capitalize on the trends. To do so, though, you must make certain that you are buying cheap . . . allow me to explain.

NETFLIX—WHEN THE MOMENTUM FINALLY RUNS DRY

If you want to understand the reason to invest in value and why never to invest in momentum stocks that are overpriced, then you need not look further than Netflix. It is perhaps the best example of why it is best to invest in value.

Netflix has been one of the more exciting stocks of the last five years (Figure 11.2). As a teacher, I can show you just about everything wrong with investing by just analyzing one stock, Netflix. It is the ultimate story of excitement about a technology that captured the minds of all investors as a next-generation company that capitalized on our desire for new technology and offered a good

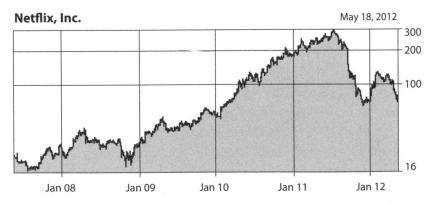

Figure 11.2   Netflix, Inc. (NASDAQ: NFLX) price performance over a five-year period prior to May 18, 2012.

service for a cheap price. You can even compare it to a bubble, much like the dot-com era, because the stock traded with exceptional momentum. It had high above-earnings movement, and then once the bubble began to deflate, the stock came crashing down with authority. This was the result of the stock being priced too high from the start.

In Chapter 10, I discussed stock metrics and how to identify healthy trading metrics for a value investment. In March 2011, Netflix was trading with a P/E ratio of nearly 70 and a price/sales ratio over 5.2, which indicated a stock that was trading way above earnings. Remember, the P/E ratio is the company's earnings per share (EPS). This is its amount of net income per share or its total number of shares. It tells you how high the company is valued over its last 12 months compared with earnings. A price/sales ratio is the same but is used with revenue rather than income. A typical value investor prefers stocks that trade with P/E ratios under 15, but I don't necessarily have a guideline for not buying stocks that trade too high above earnings. However, I use a chart similar to Figure 11.2 when talking about the P/E ratio in the fundamentals section of this book and buy stocks according to growth and how the stock measures against a P/E or price/sales ratio. These two ratios are arguably the most watched among all value investors.

With Netflix trading so high above earnings, it implies that the market was expecting earnings to continue growing at a rapid rate. A stock's P/E and price/sales ratios relate to expectations. If analysts expect a company's earnings to grow by a very large margin, the stock may trade high above earnings with higher P/E and price/sales ratios, especially if the company is exceeding expectations often. When the company does not meet expectations or in most cases does not exceed expectations by very large margins, it trades lower and sometimes loses a significant amount of its value.

In practically three months, Netflix went from trading over $300 to under $100 per share. In order to lose value to this degree, one would think that its earnings must have been cut in half. Well, that is simply not the case. Netflix actually posted an all-time best in earnings just after it began its steady trend below $100. So then you may be wondering what drove the stock so much lower.

Netflix traded lower for two reasons: a psychological change in the company's outlook and unrealistic expectations. Netflix was a craze, and given its low prices, it began an innovating service that changed the way we rented movies and enjoyed television. However, in 2011, the company had grown too large, and margins were getting squeezed, which forced the company to change its operations. The loss actually kicked into overdrive with one very simple change—a decision to split its DVD rental and streaming business into two segments with a very slight increase in price. This created anger on behalf of investors and consumers that was complemented by incredible earnings, but the earnings did not live up to the ridiculous expectations. The stock had traded from $20 to $300 in under three years as everyone tried to get a piece of the stock's bullish uptrend. No one, however, worried about patents, competition, expenses, whether it was a fad, or what would happen once its earnings slowed down.

Netflix's earnings have since slowed, and the company now faces a slew of problems. The stock's fall was very violent and hurt a lot of people who bought the stock when it was trading at metrics that did not justify an unproven platform. Stocks such as Netflix are very attractive because they rise so quickly. It's important to always remember that momentum stocks (or any stock in an uptrend) will always rise higher than they should and then will fall lower than they should. There will always be a peak at both the top and then the bottom, and as an investor in an uncertain economy, it is best for you to avoid these stocks regardless of how attractive they may appear. Don't buy unproven technologies that can become a fad. Stay away from Internet-based companies with ridiculous valuations because once growth begins to slow or something better comes along, the stocks will fall with authority and often quicker than you can react. Companies in technology and over the Internet or cloud have very few barriers to entry, which means that other companies could easily create the same products or offer the same services with ease, consequently producing an increase in competition. This can be seen in the deals industry with companies such as Groupon, Travelzoo, or Expedia or in social media because anyone can create these companies and with time and money can grow them fairly quickly. There are some who have survived and grown for a long period of time, but for every company that succeeds, there are 20 that fail. In technology, a company's time at the top with a transcendent service or device is often shorter than a career in the National Football League, and they are often overpriced. I am not saying that you shouldn't invest in technology, but I am simply telling you to watch valuations and not to get trapped into a stock that looks like a quick road to riches. They can reverse with one bad decision, and it's almost always quicker than their road to the top.

APPLE—AN EXCEPTION FOR THE MOMENT

There was a time when Nokia was one of the largest technology companies in the world and a time when Research in Motion was considered the most innovative and fastest-growing company in the market. Right now that honor belongs to Apple, but it is an honor that can change as quickly. Apple is a rare company whose 10-year 4,000 percent return is actually cheap. Every now and then you will find a stock such as Apple that trades as a momentum stock and is growing so fast that its stock is actually cheap despite such large returns.

Apple is perhaps the fastest-growing company of the last 30 years. Between 2010 and 2011, it grew revenue by $43 billion, which is larger than the market capitalizations of both General Motors and Alcoa combined during that time. Its growth has been amazing as a result of our obsession with its products, and what's even more amazing is that its growth is not slowing. We now want Apple products more than ever, and it's an ecosystem that encourages growth from other companies.

I just finished telling you to avoid the strong long-term uptrends because of their tendency to end so abruptly. However, my goal while explaining stocks such as Netflix was to identify valuation as being the most important factor when a company announces earnings because it can lead to excessive loss if earnings are weak. There are some companies that trade in a long-term uptrend like Apple but are still cheap. A stock such as Apple would not be classified as a momentum stock because the company's growth actually exceeds its stock's ability to trade higher. Therefore, you can capitalize on a stock such as Apple when it falls on dips.

One point to remember with stocks such as Apple is that it is a technology stock, and it's an industry that can change very quickly. I own shares of Apple but continue to watch it closely. Right now it may seem unimaginable for Apple to fall, but history tells us that another company, perhaps Nokia or Research in Motion, maybe even Hewlett-Packard, will develop the next big thing. At this time, Apple seems like the perfect investment with a ton of cash, great products, and a cheap stock. However, in technology, the key is to just watch because it can all change in the blink of an eye.

At this point in time, Apple is king; when the company announces earnings, it usually trades higher. In fact, since 2009, the company has only missed earnings expectations on one occasion, and it actually exceeded its own expectations, but not what analysts expected from the company. As a result, the stock has traded higher, and as earnings grow, so does the stock. Apple is a good example of a stock that continuously trades higher because it continuously beats expectations. However, what separates Apple from Netflix is its valuation. The stock trades with very healthy metrics and grows accordingly in earnings. Therefore, we are left to question whether Apple is a value stock.

Most stocks either trade with too much momentum or trade way below their worth, and this leads to periods of either significant loss or large gains. However, Apple is perhaps the fastest-growing large company in the world, and it trades with metrics that are very similar to those of Microsoft, a company that is near even in growth. Therefore, one may conclude that Apple is a value stock despite the fact that it trades significantly higher. Remember, the key to finding value isn't price or even the trend but rather the company's metrics and valuation compared with earnings. If Apple were trading with a P/E ratio of 30 and a price/sales ratio of 6, it would be trading with momentum because of good earnings. However, because Apple trades with a single-digit forward P/E ratio and a price/sales ratio that is consistent with the larger companies in the industry, this means that Apple is a value stock that trades higher according to growth. It is a very similar situation to analyst expectations. Analysts cannot accurately predict the growth of Apple; therefore, it always beats expectations. On the flip side, investors cannot buy Apple shares fast enough to match its growth, so it continues to trade with attractive metrics. As long as these variables remain consistent, Apple is still a great stock to own. As I said earlier, you must always watch for that next big thing in technology, which appears to be Apple for at least the next couple years.

HOG—USING EARNINGS TO YOUR ADVANTAGE

Sometimes you can use the insanity of earnings to your advantage to return large gains. Investors play earnings in several different ways. Some investors buy weeks before earnings statements are released, but others buy just before, hoping to capitalize on gains leading up to and then after earnings reports. Still others may short a stock before earnings, anticipating that it will fall, or even buy just after earnings are announced, thinking that it will trade higher with momentum. All these strategies require risk, but they can provide a significant upside if you are on the right side of the trade. They also can be very risky owing to the insanity of the market. However, there is one way to play earnings that is both a value strategy and allows you to truly outsmart the market by using all the tools I have discussed in this book. This involves identifying a fundamentally strong company, being patient and rational, remaining logical, identifying value, and capitalizing on its presence.

One of the absolute best times to purchase a stock and get the best price is after great earnings have just begun to fall lower. This may sound somewhat backward because stocks should trade higher following great earnings. In reality, though, this is just one more example of a flawed market that is created by humans and our irrational tendencies. It happens much more often than you would expect, and it is almost always a result of us selling without knowing why, which is something I talk about often. Knowing when and how to identify this event is when everything about identifying value and understanding market behavior comes together. To explain the technique, let me illustrate with an example of a stock I bought in 2011 following solid earnings. On October 18, 2011, Harley Davidson (ticker symbol HOG) announced quarterly earnings. The company was expected to post an EPS of $0.76. The stock had already traded lower in the preceding two months, thanks to the sell-off in the market. I identified HOG as a stock to watch before earnings because in the previous year it had increased guidance, shown signs of increased shipments, and most important, its sales were higher. Therefore, I bought a small position of 100 shares before earnings at $37.35 for $3,735, expecting it to pop following the quarter. One important point to remember is that I only bought the stock because it was already priced for value. On the next day, I awoke to the stock trading lower by nearly 5 percent; therefore, I assumed that it had posted a bad quarter.

The following hour I noticed the activity of the stock, and I analyzed the earnings report, trying to determine why it had fallen by such a large margin. I couldn't identify anything that was fundamentally wrong with its earnings. The company beat EPS expectations by $0.02, sales increased 13 percent, net income rose by 107 percent, and the company sold over 60,000 units. There was absolutely nothing I could find that could have validated why it had fallen by such a large margin. Yet, by the time I finished sorting through the data, the stock was trading with a loss of almost 9 percent.

I decided to hold my shares because I couldn't find anything substantially wrong with the earnings that would cause a 9 percent loss. If a company loses 9 percent of its valuation, I think there should be something obvious, and I still hadn't found anything. It probably wasn't 20 minutes later that the story was being discussed on CNBC, and analysts were attributing the loss to the fact that the company lowered its profit-margin forecast by 0.05 percent, citing uncertainty over foreign exchange rates. This was at the same time we were all panicking over the debt downgrade and the problems in Europe. Therefore, the media was using this cut profit-margin forecast to explain the loss, and investors were selling.

Do you remember when I was talking about humans having to find a reason for a reaction? This is why we sometimes sell to avoid further losses, but we don't really understand why we are selling. Harley Davidson is a perfect example of both events. The company had a profit margin of near 12 percent and was still selling units at a much faster pace year after year. Its stock was already fairly cheap because of the sell-off within the market, so there was no reason for a 9 percent loss if the only negative was a lowered projection of profit margins by 0.05 percent! This was not a situation such as that of Netflix or Green Mountain Coffee Roasters, where both stocks traded at more than 50 times earnings and had to be perfect on every single metric to maintain momentum. HOG was a very appropriately valued company, even undervalued, and it had just posted a phenomenal quarter by all metrics, with the exception of barely lowering its profit-margin guidance. I am not suggesting that lowering guidance is meaningless, but I am simply saying that for a stock that was already cheap, the reaction made no sense. Therefore, I purchased an additional 300 shares at $35.12 and kept the shares I already owned. This brought my total investment in HOG to 400 shares at a price of $14,271 at an average price of $35.66 per share.

To make a long story short, I held the shares of HOG for the next six months and returned a very large gain. In Chapter 12, I will be discussing how to use limits, which is the only way that you should ever buy or sell a stock. I also will explain how using limits can further eliminate emotion and allow you to become a much more profitable investor. I bought HOG because others were selling out of fear, and chances are that they didn't even know why they were selling. They just saw that the stock was falling, so they sold to avoid loss. Remember, earnings can present the absolute best of opportunities to buy a stock for value because far too often the stock will trade in the wrong direction. If you follow earnings long enough, you will notice that stocks react the minute earnings are released. Any logical investor knows that you cannot determine the success of a quarter in such a short period of time. Therefore, after my own due diligence, I bought more shares and held them to return gains. On March 26, I sold 100 shares (the first shares I bought) at $50 per share, and on May 2, I sold the remaining 300 shares at $53.50 per share for a total return of $21,050, which was a gain of $6,779, or a 47 percent gain in just six months. All I did was remain calm when everyone else was panicking for reasons they did not understand, and I acquired a very cheap, well-performing stock for a value price using nothing more than common sense.

CHAPTER 12

Eliminating Emotion with Limit-Order Trades

The investor's chief problem—and even his worst
enemy—is likely to be himself.

—BENJAMIN GRAHAM

You may not realize it, but the more engaged you are with your investments, the more likely you are to return a loss. When I first began investing, I was the worst in the world; I watched every fluctuation of a stock throughout every day. I could barely focus at work because I was so worried about logging onto my online brokerage account to see how much I had either lost or gained. If it was a day when the market fell by 150 points and I lost $300, I was selling my stocks with no questions asked, regardless of the loss.

The interesting thing about this behavior is that I would become even more frustrated as the stock would rise the following day or week because I could see the gains that I had missed. Seeing the potential gains led to desperation on my part, so I would buy as the market was trading higher and repeat the process all over again when the market turned for a day's loss.

This process is very common for an investor; in fact, most investors live in this process for years before ever even attempting to change. I completed about four to five cycles of this behavior before I stepped back, took a look at myself, thought about my actions, and realized what I was doing wrong. I realized that it wasn't my fundamental research that was causing me problems. My problems were due to my behavior and my inability to honor my research and trust that I had made a good decision. Of course, there are times when you are simply wrong. But my initial problem was that I never gave it time to see if I was right, and I never slowed down and considered the fact that the stock market is volatile, and when you own a stock, your gains/losses are going to change with every hour of the day.

As investors, we take a lot of pride in the way we choose stocks and our fundamental research. When we buy a stock, we have such high expectations that we get scared when the first thing goes wrong. This is the ultimate behavior that you are trying to change, and since you bought this book, I am fairly certain that you are familiar with the cycle. If not, then perhaps you fall into the second category of active investors who wait to sell and refuse to sell because of such strong biases toward your decisions.

Most of the time, an investor's fundamental knowledge is sufficient to return gains, but it's her emotions that get the best of her. Therefore, I wanted to develop a very simple, methodical way to eliminate all emotion associated with the buying and selling of a stock so that I could place 100 percent of my energy into my fundamental research. This simple change involved using limit orders for all of my buying and selling and setting a period of one to two years for each investment. Now I will be the first to admit that there are some times when I will trade a stock or that let my emotions get the best of me, but for 80 to 90 percent of all my investments, I use limit orders to eliminate the emotion, therefore preventing an unhealthy behavior.

USING LIMITS

One of the most significant shortcomings for investors is not fundamental analysis or even knowing how to identify an undervalued company, but knowing when to take the profits and sell the holdings. There is not a single investor who hasn't experienced a period of time when he had made substantial money from an investment and then watched it dwindled away as the stock fell. In some cases, it even returned a loss as the investor waited for the stock to rebound.

It is a normal human characteristic to never be satisfied. As humans, we always want more. Whether it is a nicer house, a newer car, or a better job, we are never satisfied and always strive to obtain more. The same is true with investments. Investors find it difficult to sell a stock that is performing well. It doesn't matter if we're up 20 percent, we will tell ourselves to hold on and wait for even larger gains. This often continues until the stock reaches its peak, but we continue to wait in hopes that it will recover, and we often lose all our gains.

The primary objective of investing is to return more money than your initial investment. Based on my experience and years of dealing with other investors, the best way to ensure gains is to use limit orders to eliminate the emotions involved in buying and selling a stock. A *limit order* is an order you can place either before or after you buy a stock that automatically buys or sells shares once the stock reaches a certain price. You can set a limit order that will expire in one day, or you can set a good-till-canceled (GTC) limit order that will remain active until it is either canceled or the order is filled. For example, if shares of Costco (ticker symbol COST) are priced at $87, you may decide after looking at the charts that it has a tendency to fluctuate between $75 and $95. Then you may want to place a limit order for $79 or even $80 because you must account for growth. To better explain this, let's look at my investment in Google (ticker symbol GOOG) and how I used limit orders to buy and sell stocks to return the largest gains by eliminating the emotions of a purchase.

GOOGLE—DOUBLING RETURNS IN A STOCK
THAT HAS ONLY RETURNED 25 PERCENT

Google was the first significantly large investment of my career. Before Google, I had invested $5,000 to $10,000 into several different companies and was able to keep a large cash position. During June and August 2008, I began to accumulate shares of Google until I had purchased 43 shares at an average price of $485 per share, which was $200 less than the stock had been priced in the prior year. Although the market was getting crushed and the fundamentals for 90 percent of all companies were being affected, Google maintained its growth and continued to post fairly impressive quarters of growth. Therefore, I felt that $485 was below its fair value considering its growth, and it most likely would not trade too much lower. Even if it did trade lower, I felt assured that the stock would recover because it was not experiencing the same difficulties.

This is a good time to reiterate the importance of price/earnings (P/E) and price/sales ratios in regard to identifying value. When I bought Google, it was trading with a P/E ratio of around 30 and a price/sales ratio of around 8, which some may think was too high considering the state of the economy. However, the company's Android operating system was catching fire, and it had good growth and a positive outlook and had traded with much higher ratios in the past. As a result, I felt as though it was a good value play because the company maintained a positive outlook and was growing at such an excessive rate despite the horrible economy. This is a good example of how value is determined not only by the trading metrics but also by a company's growth and historical trading tendencies. At $485, Google was much cheaper than it had been in the past with much better fundamentals. Looking back, I could have bought the stock much cheaper, but with this strategy I was only trying to buy low—it didn't matter whether it was the lowest point. I was just buying at a point that I know was cheap and that should appreciate in value.

During three months following my initial purchase of Google, the stock fell to a price below $300, and my loss was disturbing.

This indicates that I could have bought the stock cheaper, but I did feel as though Google was a stock that would recover because its fundamentals were still strong, and growth was imminent. When I purchased the stock, I believed that it was near its bottom. Even if it would have dropped, I had bought it with the understanding that any price under $500 was value, regardless of short-term direction. I had already decided that I would not sell but would perhaps acquire additional shares if the stock remained at such low prices. However, as rapidly as it fell, the stock began to rise. The stock reversed and was trading at over $400 within six months. Consequently, with the market in recovery or moving in the right direction, I began to think about the price at which I should sell.

At the end of 2009, Google had surpassed $600, which means that I had already attained a gain of $5,000. At this point, I considered taking profits but encountered the problem that I have been discussing. I wanted more. I did not sell the stock for a $5,000 gain, and subsequently, the stock began to fall. I watched as my $5,000 return diminished, and the stock's $610 price dropped to $580 and then to $550. I finally sold at $525. I still returned a gain of more than $1,700, but considering the volatility of the stock, I should have returned much larger gains. This is when I developed the idea of using limit orders. I still liked Google but was not willing to purchase it for more than $525 per share, the price at which I sold. Therefore, I put a limit order in to buy shares if it reached $485, which was the price I paid to buy the stock in 2008. I did not care if the position filled (was bought), but if it did, I believed that it would once again be a good value play with fundamentals improving.

Almost exactly two years after I first bought Google, in June 2010, my limit order was filled at $485. I used the proceeds I received from the sale of the stock the previous year to acquire 46 shares, three more than what I had owned before. This time, however, I was not falling into the same trap. Within days, I set a GTC limit order to sell my 46 shares of Google once it reached $600. I did not care if it took days, weeks, or months; I set the limit with the idea of holding the position for one year or until it reached $600. If not, I would reevaluate my position.

When I first set the limit order to sell Google once it reached $600, I thought it would take about a year for the order to execute. In just four months from the time I bought the 46 shares, it surpassed $600, and my order was filled. At this point, I saw the true genius of this simple strategy and decided that I would attempt to repurchase shares of Google if it dropped to $500. I believed that $500 would be insanely cheap for the stock, especially considering its constantly improving fundamentals. The reason I set the order for $500 instead of $485 was because the company had improved over the last year. So I had to account for fundamental growth and assume that the stock's bottom-level price would be higher than it was two years prior when I first bought it.

I had already kept a large cash position, so I didn't believe I was losing by not investing the money into another stock. Because value investing is all about patience, getting the best price, and identifying strong fundamentals, I was more than willing to wait for my price to be reached. I might add that most investors are unwilling to wait for a stock to reach a price with this strategy because they feel that they are losing money if they are not investing. When this strategy is used, it does more than just eliminate the emotion of buying or selling but also changes the perception and the behavior of those who are patient enough to wait and allow the volatility of the market to create the value. At this point in time, stock prices have stayed the same for the last 12 years, yet the fundamentals are constantly improving. Therefore, valuations are better. As a result, the number of value-presenting opportunities are plentiful, but in order to take full advantage, you have to remove the emotion involved with the investment or you might as well play a game of blackjack.

By the time my $600 order had been filled, I was preparing to purchase Google for the third time if it dropped to $500. I had set aside my earnings from my Google investment for a planned one year, and if the stock dropped to $500 within one year, then I would buy. If not, I would invest elsewhere. In June 2011, the stock once again fell to $500, and my limit order was executed.

After purchasing Google at $500, I decided to keep the same strategy and set a limit order for when the stock reached $600 once again. I did not have to wait nearly as long this particular time because it reached $600 in one month. As a result, I attempted the strategy once more with the belief that if something is not broken, there is no need to fix it. In August 2011, it reached $500 , and my limit order was executed for a third time, making it my fourth purchase of Google. I sold for the final time in November when it reached $600.

Following the sale of my Google shares in November 2011, the market was priced extremely cheaply owing to the sell-off. As a result, I felt that there were better opportunities elsewhere and invested my Google proceeds into Apple, a company I thought presented more upside. In a period of just three years, I returned unparalleled gains simply by eliminating emotion and allowing a system to buy and sell a fundamentally strong undervalued company.

When I first began in 2008, I purchased 43 shares, but because of the gains, I had been able to purchase 66 shares on my final investment in Google. As a result, my final return was nearly $40,000, which was nearly double my initial investment in a stock that had increased only 25 percent from the time I first purchased it at $485 per share. Now these results are not typical; usually I am only able to purchase a stock once or twice.

The important thing to remember when using limit orders is that sometimes the price will not be reached. Therefore, you must determine an allowed time for the position and then decide whether you will abandon the order and rethink your position if the order is not executed. For example, if the year had passed and my order had not been executed, then I would have moved on to another stock. Even if it was priced at $525, I still would not have purchased the stock. I would only buy at $500.

The goal of using limit orders is to eliminate emotion so that you don't deal with the "want more" attitude when it is time to sell.

This strategy eliminates the need for both buying and selling a stock, so all you have to do is find a stock that is fundamentally growing, has strong metrics, and is priced for value. In other words, it makes investing simpler and gives you one less thing to worry about while providing a more effective way to invest.

Q&A LIMITS

Over the last few years, I have spoken in detail about this particular strategy from the time I began using it. The reason is simple: There was a time when I made the same basic mistakes as everyone else, and although I still make some of the same mistakes, the occurrences are fewer and farther between. One of the primary reasons that I am such a big fan of using limits is because they assist investors in avoiding the common psychological pitfalls that I have discussed and allow investors to focus solely on fundamental analysis and finding a good entry rather than the day-to-day activity that forces them into the trap of emotional trading in the market.

For some, this strategy makes sense and will be simple to execute, but for others, it will be extremely difficult. If you are one of the thousands of investors who trade on a daily basis and try to play trends, then I believe that you will find that it is very difficult to stop. It is just like an addict who knows that his behavior is ineffective but cannot stop. Both habits impact the same part of the brain; therefore, you must treat it like an addiction and take baby steps to change the behavior. You should try using limit orders for a week or month instead of yearly and lower the desired return. As a result of heavy volatility, your order will be executed often. If you find that this is still too difficult, then create a dummy account and practice with fake money. Compare the return of your dummy account with the return on your real account. Sometimes seeing the effectiveness of a strategy is all you need to begin the process of changing a behavior.

Retail investors can be separated into several different categories according to their goals. Those who are closer to retirement or have more wealth have no problems with this strategy. For those who are trying to "get rich" in the stock market, this strategy does not satisfy the immediate gratification that many desire. Either way, this is a very simple strategy and one that I have discussed in great detail on several occasions. It is also a strategy that can be customized to meet your individual goals. Therefore, I want to take some time to answer some of the most common questions regarding using limit orders. Here are the five most frequently asked questions that should help you and make the process simpler. The important point to remember is that the strategy can be customized and that you can adjust my techniques to your personal preference and still be successful. The goal is not for you to mirror my choices but rather to become a more intelligent investor who eliminates the most common of mistakes.

Question 1: *Isn't this strategy expecting gains?*
Answer: It is a thin line between the expectation of gains that leads to emotional decisions and the expectation of gains that leads to an investment in an undervalued company. If you buy a stock, you naturally expect to return gains, or you would not have purchased the stock. However, you are not "counting" on a trend or a quick rally to return large gains. The purpose of this strategy is to allow you to focus solely on fundamental analysis and compare it with a company's valuation to determine whether or not it's over- or undervalued. For those who day trade or trade actively, they expect quick gains and chase potential gains via geek-bearing formulas. Those who use limit orders are investors who plan to invest in a company but are willing to sell if the stock reaches a level of acceptable return. Since the goal is to return more than your initial investment, this strategy makes sense because it ensures that you take profits, an action that some miss because they always want more.

Question 2: *Do you always have a set amount of time for the investment?*

Answer: Yes. I always have a set time before I manually close the position or reevaluate the position. In most cases, it is one year, but investors can decide for themselves how long they wish to hold a certain stock.

Question 3: *Do you ever have multiple limit orders on one stock?*

Answer: Absolutely! My limit orders range from one to three per investment. Presently, I am holding four different companies that I believe are presenting unprecedented value compared with current fundamentals. Therefore, I have three limit orders on each company. For the first limit order, I may sell 20 percent of the shares; for the second, I will sell 30 percent; and for the final order, I will sell 50 percent of the shares. Once again, this can be changed based on goals.

Question 4: *How do you determine the goal price?*

Answer: It depends on the company. For investments with multiple limit orders, the final order sometimes can be double the purchase price, although this is rare. These are small-cap investments or companies that are growing by large margins and trading with single-digit P/E ratios, among other factors. As a rule of thumb, I use a 20 percent gain. With this strategy, I have waited many months for the order to execute and other times only weeks. If the stock purchased truly is a value investment, my theory is that 20 percent upside is fair and achievable.

Question 5: *What about the buy price?*

Answer: I usually look at a number of factors such as the trend of the market, the price as it relates to 52-week price performance, earnings growth, and balance sheet. Anytime I decide on an investment, I research thoroughly and buy when the stock has fallen for some reason other than fundamentals. As I explained earlier, when a stock trades on an uptrend, it always reaches a peak before correcting and falling. When it is trading lower, it will bounce off the bottom before either trading higher or leveling to trade even. The goal should be to buy as it is trading lower, after it has bounced off the bottom or when it's trading flat following a downtrend. The most important point to know is whether it's a value stock. Are the fundamentals improving, does the company have a good outlook, and why did it fall? You must answer all these questions. If you establish that it fell for some reason other than fundamentals and it's priced cheap, then it could be time to buy.

CHAPTER 13

Understanding the Way You Think

Much success can be attributed to inactivity. Most investors cannot resist the temptation to constantly buy and sell.

—WARREN BUFFETT

Over the years, the practice of understanding behavioral finance has become increasingly popular because of the volatility of the market and the desire of investors to better understand how to make profitable decisions. As a result, we are now trying to understand why the market behaves in certain ways and what minor changes can be made to help investors return larger gains. The principle behind behavioral finance is to change the way you think by identifying certain behaviors and then changing them and then also to identify market behaviors that create value. Unfortunately, this can be particularly difficult because behavior is what defines us as people. Therefore, the process of changing behavior becomes a process of identifying and avoiding situations that can become triggers for us to act in certain ways.

A common belief in psychology is that identification is the first step to changing any behavior. Far too often we learn how to identify a behavior, but we don't know or don't care enough to actually change the behavior. For example, you know that eating fast food every day is bad for your health, but because it tastes good, you continue to eat the food. You know that in order to lose weight, you should eat less and exercise more, but you often "choose" not to partake in the behavioral change.

I remember one Sunday morning when I was sitting in church, and my preacher was discussing unhealthy choices and our natural instincts that prevent us from taking action. He used an example of smoking to prove his point. He said, "When you smoke, you know the health risks involved, but you procrastinate quitting because smoking may be rewarding to you at the moment." He added, "It's not like you start smoking one day and wake up with a cough, wrinkled skin, and black teeth. Because it is a slow process, smokers don't think about the consequences. When they do consider the consequences, they still make the decision to continue smoking by rationalizing and saying, 'One day I will quit' or 'I could quit if I wanted.'"

This particular sermon made me think of my grandfather. He used to always say, "If I knew then what I know now, I never would have worked at Tennessee Valley Authority, or I wouldn't have quit that job, or I would never have started smoking." I imagine that just about everyone knows someone who provides life lessons with these conversations. In reality, though, would you quit? There are several unhealthy decisions we make on a daily basis, and we continue to make the same choices because of their rewards or the rewards that we think we will receive, but then we are quick to look back on the decisions and say that we would make different choices.

The process of identification doesn't really matter if you are unable or unwilling to change the behavior. Yet both can be complex because of denial, procrastination, and emotions. This just so happens to be one of the center stones to becoming a good value investor. The process of identifying and trying to change a behavior is very similar to that of a drug addict who realizes the bad effects of his decisions but has received so much in positive reinforcement that the behavior is now a part of his life and is remarkably hard to change.

When I used to work for the Department of Corrections, part of my program was to mentally challenge prisoners to realize the impact that drugs had on their lives. Like most people, they were capable of identifying an unhealthy behavior such as being an addict, but changing the behavior and realizing the ways that drugs had affected them were the challenge. One exercise in particular was to provide scenarios that explain "a day in the life of addiction." The goal was to allow the prisoners to see the insanity of their behaviors and how the desire for drugs affected their decision-making process without having me or someone else tell them that their decisions were "insane." This would allow them to fully identify the scope of the problem while thinking rationally, which is the first step to changing a behavior.

One scenario of "a day in the life of addiction" was for the prisoners to explain their daily activities if they awoke one morning and had no money or no drugs. The question was what would you do? Would you accept the fact that you would not get your daily fix? Would you try to obtain the drugs at all costs? If so, what actions would you take?

The exercise was done in two ways, both as individuals and in a group. The individual actions were always slightly different, but the end result was usually the same. However, when asked to create an action plan as a group following the individual action plans, the prisoners surprisingly were able to compromise and agree on actions quite easily. Allow me to show you step by step the collective results of more than 500 individuals with criminal histories who woke up with no money and no drugs. This exercise also provides situational responses to each step from the instructor (me) to keep the process going.

STEP 1: Call every dealer I know in hopes that they will "front" me (which means give without payment until a later time).

INSTRUCTOR RESPONSE: No one will front. In fact, you owe several
   of your dealers money from previous fronts.
STEP 2: Look for something to sell, pawn, or trade.
INSTRUCTOR RESPONSE: What if you don't have anything to sell
   because you sold it all last week?
STEP 3: (80 percent) Call family or friends to borrow money.
INSTRUCTOR RESPONSE: What will you tell them?
STEP 4: Utilities are getting cut off or I am getting evicted.
INSTRUCTOR RESPONSE: The only problem is that your family and
   friends don't trust you, but they will call and pay the bill.
   They won't give you cash, so what's the next step? Would
   you now accept that you are not getting it?
STEP 5: Criminal activity: Responses include rob neighbor or con-
   venience store, attack drug dealer, the most popular was
   search for GPS devices, tools, or other goods in vehicles
   of random people or purse snatching.
INSTRUCTOR RESPONSE: How long does this process take?
ANSWER: Sometimes all day.

As you can see, the life and decision process of an individual
addicted to a controlled substance is quite eventful. My exercises or
studies are a good collection of data concerning the thought processes of the addicted mind. They are based on my experience with
a number of participants over a period of two years. The conversations that took place following these exercises were always intrigu-
ing because of the identification among those participating. I would
always finish with a series of discussion questions that included: Do
you ever feel bad? How often does this process occur? I would ask
their opinions on the behavior and whether they considered it normal. If not, I would ask why partake in a behavior that includes hurting others on every step and ruining your own lives.

A common misconception among the general public is that
all convicts are bad people because of actions such as the ones just
listed. However, nearly every single person I ever spoke with showed
remorse for his behavior but admitted that he could not help it.

Almost every person who took part in this exercise identified their addiction as a relationship, where drugs become their best friend. They would often acknowledge the insanity of their decisions but would justify their actions by saying that they could not help nor control it.

This behavior may seem illogical, but you must remember that what's illogical to you might be completely logical to someone else. You may wonder why someone would identify such insane behaviors but still continue doing them. The answer to this question actually lies in our brain and its relationship to choice and our desire to seek pleasure from our choices.

BRAIN BEHAVIOR

In Volume 137 of *Behavioural Brain Research*, Gaetano Di Chiara writes that over the last few years, research has shown that the relationship between the nucleus accumbens (the brain's reward center) and the behavior of investors is similar to that of addicts. You see, anytime there is an episode of desire, it is the brain's reward center that is telling our bodies to act in a behavior-seeking way to achieve a response (reward). This occurs when we are hungry. Our brain tells us that we are hungry, so we choose to eat. When we eat, our reward center supplies us with a number of neurochemicals that provide a sense of satisfaction or pleasure. This ensures that we continue to eat in order to survive. The same is true for every action we take that provides a reward. This same principle applies to other desires, such as sex. Our brain tells us we want something, we make the decision, and then once the decision is made, the brain provides a reward to ensure that we repeat the behavior. This is where the root of addiction lies. The brain tells the addict that the drug is needed to survive, and the drug then leads to excessive levels of dopamine delivered to the brain's receptors, which causes, in a sense, brain damage. But then those who partake in the activity are quick to look back on the decisions and say that they would make different choices. This process disallows the addict to receive pleasure from other activities that are not related to the use of the particular drug because the level of neurochemicals (reward) is so much greater than anything else they can achieve. It is a sick cycle, but in a nutshell, it is the cycle of addiction.

There is a strong relationship between the reward center and its functioning and the prefrontal cortex, which controls cognitive behavior. The prefrontal cortex is responsible for our decision making and our ability to decide between what's right or wrong, good or bad, risk versus reward, and the consequences of our actions. The more significant the reward, the harder it is to make a correct choice. We are a species that is motivated by emotion and pleasure. Therefore, we choose the action that provides the most amount of pleasure, or we seek that action. This helps us to understand why it is so difficult to change a behavior. In most cases, changing a behavior is an unnatural feeling that goes against the direction of our brain, making the change even more difficult.

IDENTIFICATION

In all my exercises with those addicted prisoners, I found that they were capable of identifying the insanity of their behaviors but were unable to change their behavior because of an environmental and biological desire to continue. This is not just related to addiction but to all actions in our lives that provide pleasure, a reward, or a feeling of strong satisfaction. Therefore, we can sometimes identify our unhealthy risk-taking behaviors, but when those behaviors provide positive reinforcement, we are in a mental battle between what we know is right and what our brain wants us to do. Understanding this phenomenon can help us to become better investors by helping us to identify our natural tendencies that lead to mistakes. Remember, the market is full of emotion, and emotion is bad. However, it is one of the many things that stimulate our reward center.

In "The Neural Basis of Financial Risk Taking," Camelia Kuhnen and Brian Knutson endorse this statement and take it one step further with a study concluding that activation of the nucleus accumbens preceded risky choices and risk-seeking financial mistakes, indicating excessive activation of the reward center for emotional or risky behavior. Therefore, we are encouraged to partake in risky behavior because of the reward it provides, a strong feeling of satisfaction. The goal here is to help you separate your thoughts from your actions and identify your shortcomings so that you can make a conscious effort to correct them, but you may not always be successful. To better explain this, allow me to describe my own shortcomings that lead to risky behaviors as an investor, which I have had to work diligently to correct and even still have problems with on occasion today.

The most difficult mental errors for me to overcome are the ones that involve overconfidence and excessive optimism, which go hand in hand. My wife often tells me that I am naive when it comes to people, but I call it searching for the good in everyone. I believe that every person has something that is genuinely good, but as a collection, people make stupid decisions. My desire to seek the good and overlook the bad has led me to an overly optimistic outlook on life. This is so extreme that it would become frustrating to some people. On the other hand, I have spent years in the market and have experienced unprecedented success. Therefore, I am confident in my abilities. The interesting thing is that I only got to where I am by keeping these two areas of my personality in check and realizing that any periods of emotion can lead to bad choices because, as I've learned, those periods of emotion can lead to an almost addictive behavior of seeking those feelings.

OVERCONFIDENCE

You may see this first characteristic and believe that it is a positive. After all, we are taught to be confident in our abilities, and doing so usually leads to better jobs and a more fulfilling life. However, as an investor, too much confidence can be damning to your returns.

The goal of value investing is to keep your emotions in check, which allows you to make more rational decisions based on facts, not emotion. When you are overconfident:

- You are not accountable for your decisions.
- You make excuses for why something went wrong.
- You invest with too much emotion.
- You are slow to take advice.
- You forecast.

Being overconfident is only one of many flaws an investor may exhibit that I often find myself struggling to avoid. With knowledge comes confidence, but it is important to abstain from being too confident because the market has few rules and many roads to success and failure. Therefore, you can always learn more and expand your knowledge to become a better investor.

Making excuses and not being accountable for your actions go hand in hand and are common traits of someone with too much confidence in her ability in the markets. The reason people with this problem may make excuses and not accept blame is because they feel as though they are simply too smart or that whatever caused their mishap was the result of outside forces that could not possibly be predicted. This leads us to the issue of forecasting. All investments should be made based on what we know now. We can determine whether or not a company may continue to grow, but there is no need for gaudy predictions that set you up for failure. My theory is that if I buy a company stock that is 50 percent off its fair value and it continues to grow, chances are that it will appreciate. However, you must be careful because there is a thin line between confidence and arrogance. As you can see, one pitfall can lead to numerous shortcomings that prevent you from reaching your full potential.

EXCESSIVELY OPTIMISTIC

Perhaps my greatest pitfall is my confidence, which leads to emotion because confidence and emotion are directly related. I already confessed that my wife calls it being naive, but I always look at the bright side of a situation. If the market is trading lower, I try to find the positive, such as stocks becoming cheap. Overall, I am glad that I look at life with the glass half full, and you may be too. But as an investor, you must identify and correct the problem by trying to avoid the potential problems of the emotion. If not, it can cause:

- Excitement
- Being a prisoner of the moment
- An inability to prepare for the worst
- Forecasting
- Overconfidence

You can see how my second significant weakness can affect other areas to prevent me from becoming a great investor if I allow it. These are natural tendencies that I must work hard to avoid that are a product of my environment and the behavior that I have trained my brain to honor. Being excessively optimistic leads to too much excitement, which is yet another pitfall of investing because of the limits it places on your ability to be unbiased. Someone who is particularly optimistic may become a prisoner of the moment and react irrationally to the market rather than being able to see the big picture. The perfect balance of optimism and pessimism produces the best investors because someone who only sees the upside finds it difficult to identify the downside. As a result, the person is overly confident, and that leads to unrealistic expectations.

PRACTICE MAKES PERFECT

I have built a very successful system around the notion of identifying fundamentally strong companies that are priced below fair value and then avoiding the natural pitfalls that plague me as an investor. Earlier I mentioned that it would be nearly impossible to study the entire behavior of the market because it is a machine without logic, but you can identify common trends and emotions. The emotions that you are trying to identify and profit from are the same ones that you are trying to avoid in yourself as an individual investor. Makes sense, right? The pitfalls of our own personalities are what keep us emotional, and the only way to experience a consistency of success is to avoid the tendencies that come most naturally.

You must now ask yourself the most important psychological question. Once you have identified a behavior, how do you change it? Remember, behavior is not only a product of your environment but also a survival instinct. Therefore, as I mentioned, some people won't be able to properly identify their own shortcomings because of a bias toward themselves. In the end, we as humans all individually believe that our behavior is normal. Everyone thinks that he or she is the ideal personality, and this is a gift as well as a plague.

Today I still experience the problems that I described as my own pitfalls, but my goal is to avoid these tendencies to the best of my ability. The only way to avoid them is to identify situations that spark those emotions and cause them to occur—the situations that entice our natural tendencies and behaviors to accelerate and take control of our rational thought process. The question of how to change a particular behavior is actually somewhat of a trick question. You are who you are, and that does not need to change, but the key is to control behaviors and emotions in stimulating situations that cause you to react. This is very similar to what occurs in those who suffer from addiction. The addiction will always remain, but once sober, addicts must identify the situations that causes them to relapse and then avoid those situations to the best of their ability. For investors, bad habits will remain, such as being afraid at the first sign of loss, but we can identify situations that entice emotional behavior and then avoid those situations at all cost, such as avoiding stocks with a high beta that are riskier than well-established, less volatile stocks. For example, watching your portfolio in real time, where every dollar gained and lost is immediately noticed, should be avoided because it can ignite those tendencies to overreact. It should be no surprise that with the advancements in technology, this is a common mistake that could easily lead to bad choices. With that being said, let's look at a few specific examples that most people would be better off to avoid.

QUICK GAINS

In the June 2011 issue of the *Journal of Financial and Quantitative Analysis*, research found that positive emotional states such as excitement induce people to take risks and to be more confident in their ability to evaluate an investment option, therefore indicating that excitement can lead to risky behavior and cause people to make mistakes. One of the most common ways that excitement is created in the market is by the possibility or the likelihood of quick gains.

We are all motivated by the possibility of quick gains. It's why so many people play the lottery. As investors, when we see a trend or a stock pops by 20 percent in one day, it can be very tempting to enter the position. After all, if you time it just right, you could make thousands of dollars in just one day.

For some reason, our reaction to the possibility of gains is more intense than our reaction to the possibility of a loss. This means that we don't properly assess risk during hasty decisions owing to the potential for quick gains. For those of us who are overconfident, this can be a very lethal situation. Because of our emotions, active investors very rarely consider the downside until it is realized as an actual loss. As the stock is trading higher, some investors see only the gains. When a stock trends higher by a large margin in a matter of minutes or a day, you as an investor don't have time to assess the position and make a rational decision based on the stock's positioning and fundamentals. When you buy a stock with a sudden boost, you are making the decision to buy with a totality of emotion, excitement, and without logic that is motivated by the potential for gains, not the possibility of loss.

A good example of investors chasing the quick gain was in the initial public offering (IPO) market in 2011 and 2012. An IPO occurs when a private company becomes public and begins trading in the market with the goal of raising a certain amount of cash. In

2011 (and even some in 2010), there was a boom of Internet-based companies filing for IPOs. These companies were being valued far above fundamentals and were attempting to raise amounts of money that were incompatible with their actual worth.

The reason that companies were able to begin trading with such massive valuations was that some retail investors were willing to buy their stocks regardless of valuation. One in particular was LinkedIn, a company that began trading in May 2011. It validated the market's desire to buy social media stocks regardless of their valuation and evoked memories of the dot-com bubble of the late 1990s and early 2000s.

The stock was originally priced at $45 per share, equal to a company valuation of more than $4.5 billion. This alone was considered expensive to most analysts because the company's 2010 revenue was only $243 million and its net income was $15.4 million. It gave the company a price/earnings (P/E) ratio of nearly 300 for its opening price, and remember, we know that P/E ratios of 30 are considered to be risky. Some investors justified the valuation because the company was growing revenue by 100 percent year over year, but still the company was incredibly expensive. One may even compare it to paying a million dollars for a one-bedroom condo in New York. The condo may appreciate and become a good investment depending on location, but in terms of pricing compared with all other real estate, it is very expensive.

At $45 per share, LinkedIn was valued particularly high over its earnings, but because of the IPO craze and the desperation of investors to make a quick buck, the stock climbed over 100 percent by the end of its first trading day. Therefore, the one-bedroom condo became $2 million overnight without any other factor such as a real estate boom occurring.

What retail investors don't consider is that no one was able to acquire shares of LinkedIn at $45 per share on the first day of its IPO unless the shares were bought prior to the IPO. The stock opened at $80 and then traded higher throughout the day to over $100. The reason it opened so high was because there were so many investors with orders to buy the stock once it began trading. Once again, think of the one-bedroom condo and it increasing in value overnight. We can ever add that the condo is in a great location that potentially could appreciate in the coming years. As a result, 50 people bid to buy the condo, pushing the price to over double its already expensive valuation in terms of the rest of the real estate market. In the end, though, it's still a one-bedroom condo with less than 1,000 square feet. With the same money, you could easily purchase a 10,000-square-foot home far outside the city.

LinkedIn was just one of many overpriced condos that investors were buying. This chain reaction and sense of demand have caused Internet companies to be ridiculously overvalued. Institutional investors and underwriters are running to buy high-profile Internet companies because of the massive jumps on the day of their IPOs. As a result, the rich get richer (those who could buy at around $40 per share), and the little person gets screwed (because the stock opens near its high with valuations unprecedentedly higher than earnings).

The reason it is unwise to buy a stock on the day of its IPO is that the purchase is based on pure emotion. When an investor buys a stock with the intention of returning quick gains, she does not perform the fundamental research or have a good exit strategy or plan for the possibility of loss. She is entering the position expecting to gain and therefore making it an emotional purchase. There is overwhelming evidence to suggest that seeking quick gains usually leads to loss because of an investor's emotional state throughout the duration of the investment. When we don't plan for an investment or enter a volatile situation, it leads us to contemplate our decisions and second-guess whether or not we should sell.

During the IPO craze, investors had such high expectations that relatively small gains of 5 percent were considered a failure or an unsuccessful investment. Investors typically would wait even after gains were present for larger gains. Waiting often was disastrous because of the nature of IPOs, which includes high volume and extreme volatility.

Anytime you buy a stock hoping for quick gains, you have unrealistic expectations that are complemented with emotion and a failure to consider the possibility of loss. The IPO craze is a good example, but with the number of investors who day trade increasing, this has become a particularly dangerous game of roulette. You should avoid situations such as this because they can become quite addictive and lead you to losing substantial earnings. If you feel tempted to purchase stocks that pop in premarket, IPOs, or some penny stock that promises to return immediate gains, you must then identify the behaviors that are causing you to seek these investments and not allow them to take control of your rational mind. Investments such as these are very similar to giving alcohol to an alcoholic. They change your behavior and will lead to poor performance because you will constantly chase trends rather than buy for value.

CHAPTER 14

Digging Deeper into the Way You Think

The key to making money in stocks is not to get scared out of them."

—PETER LYNCH

THE GAMBLER'S EFFECT: LUCK/SKILL RELATIONSHIP

In an article entitled, "Gambling Has Drug-Like Effect on Brain," in *USA Today*, Dr. Hans C. Breiter explores the effects of gambling on the brain. Breiter found that the parts of the brain that respond to the prospects of winning money while gambling are the same as those that appear to respond to cocaine and morphine. Furthermore, those who act abruptly in the market, chasing gains and treating the market like a poker table or, worse yet, a roulette wheel, would respond with the same parts of the brain. For many investors, this topic hits home or at least should—if you are trying to identify your own problems.

The study on gambling found that the brain uses the same circuitry for the process of diverse rewards. This topic of our brain's effect on choice is very complex and has been studied for years with various conclusions. The important thing for us to know as investors is that the brain uses the same system to produce rewards for all actions, and when we experience something pleasurable, dopamine is released, whether it's eating a steak or using cocaine. The effect of the chemical dopamine is to influence our cognitive behavior such that we continue to take part in the behavior that produces the reward, which for investors also provides a false sense of "skill."

Allow me to tell you a story that will put all of this into perspective. Back in early 2012, my wife and I spent an afternoon at the Hollywood Casino in Indiana. We had often visited the casino but usually just to eat dinner or play the slot machines. I have personally never been too fond of casinos. I think they are sad places because you often see people sitting at the slot machines dipping into their mortgage payment and just praying that they hit something big. In casinos, the possibility of winning is much more seductive than the potential for a loss, so many people who go into casinos have hopes that their prayers will be answered and that they could make a substantial amount of money. Such people rarely consider the risks.

In my opinion, there is an effective way to gamble in a casino because in a casino you are either lucky or unlucky, and if you stay long enough, you will lose. My wife and I have always operated with a particular strategy: We view a casino like a theme park, in which we are spending money for the atmosphere and the fun of the atmosphere. We take $100 each and start with all the money in our left pocket. Then anything we win we put in our right pocket. Once the money in the left pocket runs out, we cash out and go home. Thus we never leave empty-handed.

Back to the story. In early 2012, my wife and I visited the casino, but neither of us was winning at all, and our $100 each was nearly gone within an hour. I believe that I was playing blackjack, and Natalie was playing the slots. After about an hour, we decided to leave, but on our way out, Natalie saw the roulette table and wanted to play one $15 round. She had never played before, and she said that if she were to win, she would put her winnings in her right pocket, and if she lost twice, she would walk away.

Natalie got off to a good start, winning her first round. Keep in mind that she was only betting "black" or "red," which gave her a slightly less than 50 percent chance of winning owing to the "0" and "00" plays on the board. After she won the first time, she put the $15 winnings in her right pocket and then played once more—and surprisingly, she won! She then played again, and again, and again and won each time, now five times in a row.

By this time Natalie was five and zero and had won $75, and she began to believe that there was some level of strategy to her success or that she could "feel" where the ball would land next if she walked away from the table, didn't watch, and went with her first instinct. She then went on to win, win, win, and win again. Now she had won nine times in a row, and she was $135 ahead, and she was convinced that there was some level of skill involved. On her tenth attempt, she lost, yet she still had one more round and was convinced that she had lost only because she did not go with her initial choice.

Natalie continued with her good fortunes and won another seven times in a row before losing. Thus she had won $240. As we left, Natalie felt particularly confident that her winnings were the result of talent and that when she lost, it was because of some outside reason or because she did not trust her initial instincts. She believed that she shared certain connections with the dealer, the speed at which he spun the ball, and that the atmosphere all played a role in her doing the statistically impossible. Yet the truth is that if she won 16 times and only lost twice, then most likely someone else experienced the opposite fate, winning only twice and losing 16 times.

Natalie's thought process is nothing unusual. In fact, everyone who goes to a casino shares these beliefs (when they're winning). This is due to the perfect mixture of excitement and the possibility of money-earning activities. In reality, though, there is no skill involved. Natalie was simply lucky. Yet this is hard for some people to accept. Such people go to a casino, sit at a specific slot machine, play only with a particular dealer, and develop a strategy that gives them the illusion that all money-earning activities are the result of strategy rather than luck.

We do this when we trade stocks. Any time those behavioral and pleasurable regions of the brain are stimulated from money-earning activities, it is in our nature to try to find a reason for the win, develop a strategy, and relate the success to skill so that we believe the same level of excitement or reward can be created at a future date. I often compare this example of my wife to that of a day trader. Now there are many people who make a living as successful day traders, and I like to call them "poker players" because obviously there is some level of skill involved in poker, and for a trader who studies trends and spends all day looking at charts, it is possible to develop a system that works better than 50 percent of the time. However, the two—a poker player and a day or situational trader— have striking similarities.

When a great poker player wins a tournament or plays well, then it's because he or she is talented or the best at playing poker. Yet, if the same person loses, it is because of "bad hands," one mistake that could've been averted, or some other outside reason that doesn't suggest that the game is in many ways based on luck. The same is true for day or situational traders; they spend days looking at a chart and identifying certain technical indicators that tell them that a stock will "break out." If the stock does break out, then it's because of pure skill. Yet, if the stock trades lower, then it is because of an economic situation, a company development, or some other outside reason that acted beyond the scope of the trader's belief and forced the stock lower. Therefore, the loss was not due to luck or the fact that the stock had a 50 percent chance of trading higher or lower on any given day. Basically, the trader will avoid any and all explanations that could challenge his or her "skill" to call the day-to-day trends of a stock. In fact, traders rarely realize that they call just as many wrong trends as correct ones. This is so because in order to keep the brain satisfied, the dopamine rolling, and the excitement building, we must take credit and convince ourselves that there is some measureable strategy to follow that will allow us to experience these pleasures once more, even if the large return on the stock or the roulette game was nothing more than pure dumb luck.

MIND, BODY, AND RISK

Aside from our need to find a skill level for any money-producing actions, there is also a biological factor or a mind/body relationship that also aids in this process. There is strong scientific evidence that suggests that the prospect or anticipation of financial gain triggers a flurry of dopamine activity similar to that of an addict. These high levels of dopamine create a desire to make emotional decisions in the same way an addict must continue to take more drugs to achieve the same "high." A person who makes such emotional decisions must place riskier bets to receive the same level of satisfaction. In "Genetic Determinants of Financial Risk Taking," Camelia Kuhnen concludes that the more money that was available to participants, the more money they invested in risky investments over safer investments. When the potential for a large return was present, the investors were willing to take larger risks, further showing the stimulation that we seek for large returns or a quick buck and how the potential for large returns often can cloud our judgment. One problem is that such an investor does not realize the desire for this reward, and it also prevents him or her from having the ability to assess risk. A good example of this action occurred during the initial public offering (IPO) craze involving social media stocks, which led to risky behavior or buying significantly overvalued stocks for the possibility of returning quick and large gains.

At this time, there is little evidence to explain why this reaction occurs. In fact, we don't even know for certain why the anticipation of gains, not the realization of gains, causes us to become so excited. I suspect that it's because when we anticipate gains, we are overconfident or excessively optimistic. Such traits I identify as weaknesses. These weaknesses are prevalent in most investors because investing is a proud industry where everyone believes that he or she is correct and that he or she is making intelligent, well-thought-out decisions.

It is common sense that you wouldn't purchase a stock expecting to lose, so the goal of investing is to return more than your initial investment. At the same time, no one really knows how the market will perform or if earnings for a particular company will continue to grow at a rate that is acceptable to investors. Therefore, when I purchase a stock, I don't think of it as a get-rich investment or an investment for a quick gain. Rather, I see it as an investment of value. When I buy, I do assume that the stock will trade higher, but I try to eliminate the natural bias that arises from purchasing a stock, and I purchase with the understanding that the stock is undervalued at the time.

As I mentioned earlier, we are all somewhat biased toward the investments that we choose. I constantly remind myself that nothing in the market is guaranteed, and then I put myself in the best possible situation by buying stocks that are cheap compared with current fundamentals. The trick is not to expect but to plan for the worst and hope for the best by buying stocks that you know are currently cheap. Then eliminate as much emotion as possible using limit orders and emotionless trading. Basically, have a plan before you purchase the stock. Tell yourself that you are not buying until it reaches x price, and then you will set a limit order to sell once it reaches y price. This eliminates emotion and is based on fundamental analysis that disallows you from activating the chemicals in your brain associated with pleasure by simply limiting your involvement in the purchase and sale of the stock. In Chapter 15, I will discuss this process in detail, and you will see how I have used this strategy to eliminate the drawbacks of my own personality.

REALIZATION OF LOSS

In *The Little Book of Behavioral Investing*, James Montier explains a common behavioral misstep of investors, based on an original study by Terrance Odean in *Are Investors Reluctant to Realize Their Losses*, which perfectly explains the way that we as investors perceive a loss and our misconception that a stock will "bounce back." This is a problem that I often discuss. We are sometimes so confident in our knowledge that we never suspect that we could make a mistake or we believe that our investment decision is so good that although the stock is down, it will almost certainly rise at some point. Therefore, the results from Odean's study makes sense. He examined the data from roughly 10,000 investment accounts from 1987 to 1993 and arrived at the conclusion that investors held losing stocks an average of 124 days versus holding a winning stock only 102 days. Further research indicated that retail investors are 1.7 times as likely to sell a stock with gains versus a stock with loses.

Investors are typically confident in their abilities and find it difficult to consider the potential for loss when they purchase a stock. Sometimes you will do all your homework with fundamental analysis and enter the position at the best possible price, but the stock still will fall and never appreciate in the set time you have allowed for the investment. Unfortunately, this is a reality of the stock market. Sometimes you are going to lose, and it doesn't mean that you made a bad investment, but it validates the fact that it is impossible to be right 100 percent of the time.

Given our natural bias for a particular company that we like, it is very difficult to avoid the anticipation of gains. When we anticipate gains, dopamine is overloaded into our brains and clouds our cognitive reasoning. You would think that the same thing would occur with loss, and it would provide an equally stimulating experience. In reality, though, it is the opposite. Our brain actually becomes less active when faced with loss. In fact, the realization of loss was identified on the left hemisphere of the brain, whereas the response to winning was located on the right, further showing the distinction in how we identify both events.

To better understand our reactions to winning and losing, think back to the casino: Natalie was more than willing to believe that her winning was due to skill, but when she lost, she believed that it was due to outside forces and responded with complete opposite emotions. For example, after her big day at the roulette table, Natalie all of a sudden wanted to start going to the casino more often and always wanted to play roulette. However, her results were never the same, although her behavior had changed. She was no longer as nervous, and rather than placing the minimum $15 bet, she would bet $20 or $25, which she needed in order to provide the same reward she received during her winning streak.

Natalie is a good example of the process, but nowhere near as close an example as the couple we took to the casino following Natalie's lucky day. This is so because Natalie is by nature more conservative and is the type of person who can't stand to "blow money" that she could possibly give away to people who need it. Our friends who went to the casino with us, on the other hand, are much different. The man, who I'll call Kevin, is more seeking of quick gains, the type of person who often buys and resells stocks or looks for a quick and easy way to make money. Therefore, he would be much more stimulated by winning and more likely to increase his level of risk taking to meet his pleasure needs.

To make a long story short, my wife and I and our two friends (one being Kevin) went to the casino to get dinner and play some slots. During dinner, Natalie explained to Kevin how she had won over $200 playing roulette and how she believed that it was due to some sense of skill (despite the fact that she'd not experienced the same level of success). I attempted to explain that she was wrong, but Kevin was hooked, and you could see his mouth watering and the excitement in his eyes at the pure thought of winning, not considering the potential for loss.

It's also important to know that Kevin and his fiancé were in college and did not have a great deal of money, so we were taking them out for a good night on the town. I believe that we stayed at the casino for about three hours. Natalie and I used our strategy of putting winnings in one pocket and our bank in the other. Meanwhile we told Kevin and his fiancé about our strategy to avoid total loss, but they would not listen, and the emotions of the gamble took over. Kevin stayed at the roulette table, winning about 40 to 50 percent of the time, and by the time we left, he had lost more than $150, which is not a great deal of money, but when you're in college, it's a lot.

Almost immediately we noticed Kevin's and his fiancé's mindset change, and they were depressed to have lost the money. However, like many others, neither could accept the loss, and they were excited by the casino's atmosphere. Therefore, they rationalized that if they went to another casino, perhaps they would do better. As a result, after we got back to our house, at midnight, Kevin and his fiancé left and did not return until 4:30 a.m., obviously having better results.

When they awoke the next day, at about 1:00 in the afternoon, Kevin couldn't quit talking about his strategy on roulette that was a guaranteed win. He had won over $150 the night before and believed that his strategy would give him more money in the future. Remember, he is the type of person who chases quick money or the possibility of quick money.

Kevin's strategy was to bet red or black and then also two-thirds of the table with two of the three rows. The red or black bets pay double, but when you bet one of the three rows, you get three times your bet. Thus, if you bet $15 on the first row (one-third of the board), you would win $45. Therefore, Kevin's goal was to bet $15 on red or black and then $30 on two rows, therefore making his total bet $45 and increasing his chances of winning to almost 85 percent.

Immediately after I heard Kevin's plan, I started to poke holes in his strategy, but just like the night before when he did not listen about only playing a certain amount of money (right pocket, left pocket), he did not listen this time. He did not realize that because of the amount he was betting, he would have to hit both the correct color and one of the two rows to earn 65 percent on his bet. Therefore, he is betting a large amount, $45, but could only win $30 best-case scenario. If one of his two rows wins, then he breaks even, and if red or black wins (and nothing else), then he loses $15.

Kevin's winnings were a result of choosing both the correct color and one of the correct rows the night before, and because of his strategy, his chances of winning were greater, but not that much, and one loss results in a $45 hit. Kevin decided, against all advice, that his strategy was so solid that it was worth taking the day off, and rather than taking his winnings from the night before, he decided to go back and try to win more easy money. This behavior is one of the primary reasons that investors lose money. They may have large gains, but greed and the desire for more causes them to wait for even larger gains, and their confidence overshadows reason, which is what happened to Kevin.

The end result of Kevin's strategy was that he not only lost all his winnings from the night before, but he also lost an additional $150. His excitement turned to depression because he'd already taken the day off and had lost all his gains. He not only continued to play his strategy, but because three total losses would be near $150, he also began to bet $25 and $35 on red or black, with his goal being to "win back" his money. This story brings truth to the expression that every loser in Vegas thinks they can do better, but the winners leave the table when they are up. But it is also a prime example of common investment mistakes. If you trade stocks, then you must acknowledge that you have a 50 percent chance of gaining or losing. As with poker, there is some skill involved in technical trading, but you also must acknowledge the losses and must take notice following those losses with the same intensity that you show when you gain. The only difference between trading the market and playing a roulette table is that the market does not have any consistencies. In roulette, you know the return when you pick a color. But you don't know the return when you buy a stock to trade, and since trading requires riskier, more emotional behavior, the gamble must constantly evolve and become larger in order to achieve the same reward. In short, it is the process of not being able to accept responsibility for loss but being willing to accept full responsibility or credit for gains and then doing whatever it takes to repeat the behavior and to achieve the reward that is provided with this behavior.

The inability to accept loss and the anticipation of gains go hand in hand. You should have a proper exit strategy before you enter any position. However, with riskier investments such as IPOs and spur-of-the-moment purchases, it is impossible to develop an appropriate exit strategy. You must realize that the desire to buy promising penny stocks or IPOs may create the illusion of quick gains that in some cases may change your life but never actually provide the reward of large gains.

I know that your expected gains finally could allow you to purchase that boat you've always wanted. More than likely, though, you won't return gains. If the buy does present gains, you most likely won't sell the stock because your expectations are too high, and you want your anticipated gains. Therefore, you wait too long and don't consider the possibility of loss. Once you do sell for a loss, you become desperate. Consequently, you start making riskier decisions just to make back the money you lost, and you lose even more money. It is a sick cycle, my friend, and it is the behavior of a compulsive gambler. Unfortunately, the market is full of compulsive gamblers, and it can be easy to follow the crowd, unless you can identify and avoid the behavior with well-thought-out and intelligent decisions.

CHANGE THE WAY YOU THINK

One of my primary goals when I worked for the Department of Corrections was to give inmates both short- and long-term goals that they actually wanted to achieve. The reason this was so important is that addicts or people with addictive personalities have trouble delaying gratification. It is one of the reasons that drugs became a part of their life. They had trouble planning and achieving long-term goals because they only worried about satisfying the moment. Investors possess these traits as well; we always want the quick fix and want to buy the stock that is on the solid uptrend, but we do not think about the stock's chances of falling. It is these patterns of behavior that create opportunity for value investors and allow us to see potential gains in areas that are undiscovered and undervalued.

Our behaviors are something we spend a lifetime creating. They are the result of cause and effect from the rewards provided from certain behaviors and our ability to learn from our mistakes. Investing can be very rewarding, but regardless of your success, it is most important to remain calm and act without a sense of emotion and/or urgency. Unfortunately, you can't eliminate all emotion, nor can you eliminate all bias. However, you must identify which areas of your personality may become problematic and then avoid those situations like an alcoholic has to avoid places where drinking occurs.

Perhaps the most significant trap that plagues investors is the expectation of gains. After all, if you buy a stock, you expect it to return gains. There are simply too many investors with short-term day-trade philosophies that offer unrealistic goals. Such an expectation or, as I call it, sense of entitlement leads to emotional decisions and anticipation of immediate wealth. Consequently, these emotional decisions lead to a change in the investor's behavior in which fundamental analysis becomes trend seeking, which ultimately leads to desperation and failure as an investor.

One of the ways that I have found to eliminate emotional purchasing and to keep rational goals is to limit my involvement in the trading of stocks. This means being active but also passive as an investor, as well as being able to avoid the tempting lures of the market's momentum stocks. In Chapter 15, I will show you in detail from my own experience how to eliminate emotion by preparing for the sale of a stock before you buy it. Remember, one of the largest problems for investors is taking profits and waiting too long to sell. If your goal is to return profits and you are truly purchasing stocks of value, then you should return gains most of the time. By watching the stock on a daily basis or trying to play the trends, you are only gambling. If the only way to change your behavior is to avoid the behavior, then you must change the way you buy and sell stocks.

PART IV

CHAPTER 15

Most Valuable Lessons Come from Loss

A big part of being strong financially is that you know where you are weak and take action to make sure you don't fall prey to the weakness. And we ALL are weak.
—DAVE RAMSEY, FINANCIAL EXPERT, AND AUTHOR

Even with proper execution of every trade, there will still be times when you make mental errors or return a loss. There is no way to experience gains 100 percent of the time, but you can decrease the number of occurrences that return a loss and significantly improve your overall return if you take the time to identify your behaviors and, more important, learn from your experiences as an investor.

One of the most unlikely success stories comes from one of my larger investments during the recession. It unfolded from a purchase I made near the lowest point of the financial recession in 2009. Up to that point, I had been successful at trading the ups and downs in the market but was still losing money like everyone else during this two-year span. However, I kept my eyes open for companies that I believed were undervalued, like Google, and I was prepared to use the period as a way to load up on cheap stocks.

CITIGROUP: MY BEST TRADE

Throughout the recession, there was one stock that I watched with pure amazement, and it was Citigroup. I was amazed at the rate at which the stock dropped over a period of two years. I would play little games with Citigroup and try to determine how much lower it could fall, and it just kept falling beyond my wildest dreams. It went from $55 to $31 in less than six months, only to free fall to under $20 less than four months later. I was amazed at this volume because although I knew the financial situation in the United States, I was still unable to process the speed of loss for one of the world's largest financial institutions.

At $20 a share, I almost pulled the trigger, but just before I did, the stock dropped again and pretty much continued until it reached a price of $1. During this time of great fear, I strongly believed that the stock was presenting value, and at $1 a share, it was offering an unprecedented level of value. Yet I still decided to wait with the intention of eventually purchasing the stock to capitalize on its low price.

The stock began to rise in March. It went from $1 to $2 and then ultimately $3 in one month's time. At that point I was feeling good and confident that an investment in Citigroup would provide me with large gains and a stock that was sure to at least reach $20. I mean even at $20, it was still going to be trading with losses of great proportions. Therefore, I decided on a somewhat large position in the stock. If you remember, I had already owned stock in Google, but in the past, my investments were somewhat small considering the metrics of an investment in Wall Street. With Citigroup, I believed that because of its loss, the stock would recover with large gains from $4 per share, and it was an opportunity I could not pass up. However, this investment would be much different from my investment in Google because Citigroup was not a company with fundamental improvement and a fallen price. Instead, the company was largely responsible for the conditions of the market and operated with a great deal of uncertainty.

After assessing my risk versus reward, it seemed logical to initiate a position in Citigroup. I invested a fairly large position because the stock was then trading higher and had fallen to lose almost all its value. I set an order to purchase 4,000 shares when it crossed the $4 price, which happened on May 8, 2009. Keep in mind that this was around the same time that my already large investment in Google was trading at under $400 before I developed my limit-order strategy. Google had begun to recover along with the rest of the market, so I believed the timing to be perfect because I thought that we were now in recovery mode and that the large banks, with Citigroup being the most undervalued, would recover with large gains.

I will never forget the moment that my Citigroup purchase was initiated. I was the happiest guy on the face of the earth because I just knew that I had made an investment that was going to provide a 500 percent return within one year. At the time, the stock had risen 400 percent in less than three months after it had dropped from nearly $60 in two years. In my mind, I only looked at the price of Citigroup. I was emotionally attached to the thought of returns that were too good to be true and purchased a stock that I did not fully understand. In retrospect, this is a problem that I have identified in most retail investors. At this point, I was not a rookie, and prior to the recession, I had become successful as an investor and felt exceptionally confident in my abilities, which is yet another of my pitfalls that I have described. Yet my belief that I had found the diamond in the rough clouded my judgment, and the potential for gains caused me to become emotional, which is a deadly combination for an investor.

It wasn't one week later that the stock began to drop. I watched as my $4 stock dropped to $3.50 and then to $3 over the next month. I was flabbergasted, speechless, and in shock after I had invested so much into this one security because I was counting on it for my quick road to riches. Although I had experienced a similar situation with Google, it was different because my Google investment was trading higher, and I was forced to watch Citigroup trade lower while others traded higher. Since Citigroup was not a company with improved fundamentals, my fear kicked into overdrive.

By this time, the analysts had turned on the stock and had gone from talks of recovery to talks of a continued fall. My optimism quickly turned to panic and fear that overtook my rational thought process, what little I had left. The stock continued to drop and was now lower than $3. It was approaching $2.75 and then $2.70, so finally I couldn't take anymore and pulled the trigger. I decided to sell my road-to-riches security for a 30 percent loss.

At first, I felt much better after selling the security because the stock continued to fall below $2.50. However, just as abrupt as the security fell, it began to rise once again in the same manner as it had fallen to a price of over $5. My feelings of relief from selling the stock now left me feeling sick. I lost over $5,000 when I could have gained $4,000, a difference of $9,000, if I would have just hung on.

LESSON LEARNED

If you don't profit from your investment mistakes,
someone else will.
— JEFFREY A. HIRSCH, *STOCK TRADER'S ALMANAC 2012*

Looking back, I understand the mistakes that I made. My assumption was that Citigroup offered value, when I never once considered why Citigroup had fallen, and I never looked at the company's fundamentals or toxic assets, nor did I consider the economic issues that directly affected this financial institution. I made an investment on the pure fact that the stock was cheap and that it had lost a large amount of value in a short period of time. Before the recession, Citigroup was not one of the stocks that I had studied with any intensity, and I was not very knowledgeable regarding the company's operational issues. If I had spent a little more time and due diligence, I would have known that the company was writing mortgages with its eyes closed and was lucky to have the valuation at $1 per share.

At the time, I was disgusted and sick by the amount of loss I experienced during such a short period of time. Now I have used it as a learning experience and decided to correct the mistakes that I made with this investment. Although I believed that I was investing for value, I was not. I invested because of the price of a stock with no regard for its fundamentals or its psychological value. I am often asked about the best investment I ever made. Usually, when people ask this question, they are interested in knowing about my largest return in a single day or my largest return on a single investment, but I don't tell them about the large returns. Rather, I cite this particular investment, which allowed me to experience my largest loss to date. I always tell them about my purchase of Citigroup because I learned more about myself and my investment strategy there than with any other stock that I have ever purchased.

KEEP TRACK

Some who experienced my fate with Citigroup would not have been so pleased with the result. I guess this is where my ability to look on the bright side of life pays dividends. My goal is that with each investment I can learn and become a better investor. Obviously, Citigroup and Google were special in helping me to develop as an investor. Honestly, both investments could have been interpreted in a different way. I could have just as easily looked at Citigroup as a failure and become desperate in trying to "win" my lost money back. In such a case, I would have learned nothing and probably would have lost even more. With Google, I could have easily looked at the lost gains from my first investment because it reached $610 and then fell before I sold at $525. I could have been discouraged and moved on to the next investment. Consequently, if I hadn't learned from both experiences, it is very possible that I wouldn't be in the position that I find myself in today.

I attribute all my success to my ability to reflect, identify my shortcomings, and learn from my mistakes. I am not an overly intelligent person who is smarter than everyone. However, I am patient, and I have used all my experiences as learning tools. With that said, how many potential learning experiences have you ignored? Do you know all your investments for the last year? If so, what did you learn?

When I worked for the Department of Corrections, I was often told to "document everything!" The reason for this was the clientele we served. They were always trying to scheme or use one staff member to get what they wanted, so we all had to be on the same page. There were 60 of them and only 8 of us, so it was important that we document every encounter or problem that would be important for others to know about.

Back in 2009, I decided to begin documenting all my investment transactions. At first, it seemed irrelevant because my brokerage firm kept everything on record, but I found out over time that the notes I was writing became important documentation that recorded all my thoughts about a particular investment. My notes reflected what I learned, what I did right, and what I did wrong. I also kept track of gains and losses for a particular investment, and I wrote down any information I gained from the trades that might be useful in the future.

Throughout this book I haven't told you anything that you *have* to do to succeed. I have suggested a lot of different strategies or techniques that I have used to return gains. I have also explained emotion, fear, panic, fundamentals, and so on, but I have been loose about all the information by saying I don't expect everyone to use limits or by acknowledging that there are several ways to make money in the market. It doesn't have to be my way. My personal goal for writing this book is for you to be able to take something from it and incorporate it into your own investment strategy to return larger gains or learn what I consider to be the right way to invest if you are just starting off. I figure that if you can return an additional 5 to 10 percent per year, then the $25 price of this book is well worth it. But one thing I am telling you that you must do that will drastically improve your returns is to keep a journal or a folder on your computer that details all your thoughts and experiences with every stock you buy, including why you bought it.

You may not think writing investment information could serve a beneficial purpose, but you would be wrong. Keeping a journal is one of the best ways to reflect on your successes or failures, and it helps to identify any problematic behaviors that you may not notice. You should be able to record why you purchased a stock, why you sold it, how many shares you held, and your overall gain or loss, along with any other feelings or thoughts related to the buy or sell of the stock. With that said, let's look at five benefits to using an investment log:

- **Trading activity.** Sometimes we as investors forget the reasons that we began investing. Our actions fail to reflect our goals, and we start making decisions that are hasty and outside our comfort zone. We become emotional investors, and then we let all reason and rationale go out the window. By documenting all your thoughts and actions, it is easy to stay on track because you will see over the course of several years the results of your actions and which actions lead to problems and which result in success. Therefore, if you're ever tempted, which is normal, it is easy to be reminded with a detailed log of your trading activity.
- **Eliminate temptation.** By writing down all your thoughts and actions, you are able to realize your behaviors and draw conclusions that you may otherwise not notice, which makes it easier to avoid hasty decisions that do not fit into your goals.
- **Accountability.** If you write down all your thoughts related to your investments along with the reasons for the buy or sell, then you will not be able to blame the loss on outside forces, and you will be able to recognize the reasons for your success. You have to be accountable for your actions, and you can identify why you made certain choices and learn from those choices without excuses.

- **Progression.** You should learn something from every investment. By writing down the notes from a holding, it will be easier to evolve, get better, and keep from making the same mistakes.
- **Education.** Perhaps this is the most important benefit. Investors are naturally drawn to certain investments over others, and an investor will sometimes buy the same stock several times over a period of a couple years. If you document well, you will be able to look back at notes for a previous investment and find information that may help you the next time.

Taking notes serves a multitude of purposes. The ones just listed are only a few. You can write down anything you desire that might be of help to you later. After all, we are always trying to learn from our mistakes, build on what works, and become much better investors regardless of market conditions.

CHAPTER 16

What Offers Value?

When stocks are attractive, you buy them. Sure, they can go lower. I've bought stocks at $12 that went to $2, but then they later went to $30. You just don't know when you can find the bottom.

—PETER LYNCH

At this point, I am in the process of putting everything together. By now, you should understand fundamentals and be able to identify certain behaviors that can affect your performance and your concepts of value. However, it can still be difficult to piece everything together in a way that creates a solid foundation for success. Therefore, in these final three chapters, I am going to lay out a guideline that I have used to become successful. The neat thing is that you don't have to follow my exact guideline, but you can find parts that work for you and then incorporate the ideas into your own strategy. My goal is not to change everything about your investment style but rather to challenge what you believe is correct and allow you to make your own decisions once you see a few alternative methods.

TEN-TEN-TO-TEN FORMULA

A few years ago, I set out to develop a system that would allow me to find value on a consistent basis and would return gains most of the time. What I found is that such a system does not exist, and if someone tells you that such a system does exist, then you should run. In the market, there are no 100 percent guarantees. You can do all your homework and put yourself in the absolute best situation and still be wrong. However, in 2010, I created and began using what some now call the *ten-ten-to-ten system*. This system was created with the idea of finding the perfect balance of growth, valuation, and performance to ensure that you are not buying too high and that you are buying a fundamentally growing company. The term *ten-ten-to-ten* refers to 10 percent for all three of the measured metrics that in theory would suggest a perfectly valued company. Therefore, inconsistencies can indicate a stock priced too high or too low.

The system takes into account three very basic measurable items—price/earnings (P/E) ratio, earnings growth, and stock performance—by allowing you to see how a company is currently valued compared with its growth. Now I must add that no due diligence should be complete with a system this simple. However, this system can help to eliminate certain companies as potential buys and allow you to separate out companies that are presenting value. Therefore, you can research other areas of growth and spend more time looking at other important metrics. However, one fact that I have found to be true is that there is such a thing as too much research. It can cause you to contradict yourself and allow one negative to overshadow 10 positives. Just remember, a stock is kind of like a spouse—they all have flaws, but hopefully you can make the best all-around choice with the fewest number of flaws. As a result, you can use the ten-ten-to-ten system to identify which is the cheapest stock in terms of performance to valuation to growth.

In theory, a company with 10 percent growth, a P/E ratio of 10, and a one-year return of 10 percent would be fairly valued. Hence a company with 10 percent growth, a P/E ratio of 20, and a one-year return of 5 percent would be a stock that is overvalued compared with its growth (P/E ratio greater than year-over-year earnings growth) and a stock that is now posting slower returns in terms of performance. Therefore, the stock could quit returning gains until the three metrics are balanced or are at least in the same proximity. The truth is that I could write an entire book discussing this one strategy, and a whole book probably would be necessary to achieve a detailed explanation of its purpose. However, at this point, the strategy should be used only to find inconsistencies and to compare a company's valuation with its growth. You also can add to the metrics used and incorporate revenue growth to get an even better sense of valuation. Let's take some time to look at some examples (see the following table) to show you how this can help in identifying a potentially undervalued company.

COMPANY	TICKER SYMBOL	EARNINGS GROWTH (2010–2011)	P/E RATIO	ONE-YEAR RETURN
Apple	AAPL	85 percent	13.75	65 percent
Microsoft	MSFT	23 percent	10.40	20 percent
Lululemon Athletic	LULU	50 percent	54.72	60 percent
Intuitive Surgical	ISRG	30 percent	39	50 percent
Under Armour	UA	41 percent	51	10 percent
Foot Locker	FL	64 percent	15	26 percent
Panera Bread	PNRA	30 percent	30	17 percent

The first area you always want to look at is the company's earnings growth. Second, you compare it with the stock's one year return. If the company's earnings are growing faster than its stock (as with Apple), this tells you that the stock is even cheaper than it was last year despite a yearly return. This situation is the perfect scenario and exactly what you seek as a value investor. In fact, Apple has had so many years of posting earnings that grow faster than its stock that its P/E ratio is under 14, similar to a company that is posting flat or minimal growth.

Another point to consider is that when a company grows larger, its metrics decline in size. You don't see too many $100 billion companies with P/E ratios of 100 (except Amazon), so as a company grows larger, the P/E ratio becomes less relevant (assuming that it's under 16), and the company's earnings growth compared with stock performance becomes most important. My theory is that I always want to see a large company post higher earnings growth compared with stock performance, as with Microsoft. Even though its growth was only 23 percent year over year compared with a 20 percent yearly stock return, its P/E ratio is 10.4 (which is very low even for a large company). This indicates that the company's stock is moving according to earnings, yet over time the stock continues to get cheaper as it grows, which is a phenomenon that should occur. It indicates that the stock is moving in the right direction.

In the case of Lululemon, the company's stock is moving faster than its earnings. This means that its P/E ratio also will continue to increase, and the stock will become more expensive. Theoretically, if the company were trading with 50 percent earnings growth, a 50 percent return, and a P/E ratio of 50, then it would be priced better for fair value. As value investors, we would not be willing to buy unless the growth exceeds the return, and the P/E ratio is less than the year-over-year growth. For example, 50 percent growth, a P/E ratio of 45, and 45 percent return would be much more attractive. Remember, when considering value, you must take into consideration the company's growth. It's not all about P/E ratios, although they are very important.

Intuitive Surgical trades with a P/E ratio far above earnings growth, and its stock is growing nearly 70 percent faster than its earnings. This indicates that the stock is not only overvalued but also could experience a period of years where it either sees no return or even trades significantly lower. Even then it still may be overpriced. Under Armour is an example of what I expect from Intuitive Surgical in the next couple years, possibly sooner. Under Armour experienced several years where the stock grew much faster than earnings. As a result, the company is still growing by 41 percent year over year, but its stock rose only 10 percent last year, allowing

the P/E ratio and the growth of earnings to match more closely. You can see with 41 percent earnings growth that the company still has quite a wait before its value will reflect its earnings. So basically UA could be a meaningless hold unless your goal is no return.

Foot Locker, on the other hand, is a perfect example of an undervalued stock with growth that far exceeds value. Foot Locker's earnings are growing more than double the speed of its stock price, and its P/E ratio is less than 25 percent of its earnings growth. This indicates that the stock could experience a very long uptrend and return very large gains. I am not suggesting that it could carry a P/E ratio of 60 because all industries are valued differently, but at its current valuation, it is very possible that it could now grow with earnings, maintain its current P/E ratio, and still be considered undervalued.

Panera Bread, in my opinion, is fairly valued, perhaps a little undervalued, and if it continues on this route, it could become a great value investment in 2013. In this case, the company's 30 percent earnings growth and its P/E ratio of 30 are near the benchmark for the ten-ten-to-ten strategy. Its one-year return of 17 percent shows the correction that took place in its shares, which is what will most likely occur in shares of Intuitive Surgical, Lululemon, and Under Armour. Now that the company's valuation matches its growth, the stock can trade with more consistency and be more rewarding to its shareholders. I would not call it a value investment but rather a fairly valued investment.

Let's say that you are considering three potential investments. You like each company equally and believe that they would all make good investments. You think each is priced well, but then you use this very simple formula, and it eliminates one. You can then perform additional due diligence to determine whether or not both companies are expanding and operating efficiently, and you can perform a comparison of their balance sheets or cash positions in order to determine which is the best. Sometimes investing can become overwhelming with so much information that it is nearly impossible

to cover each aspect of a company, especially because changes in the market happen so speedily. This formula is to serve as a starting point and is something I have used for the last few years to find companies with earnings growth that far exceeds stock performance.

Before I conclude the discussion of this strategy, I want to show you an example of how this strategy works. The examples I just explained are stocks at their current positions that I used to determine whether any could be presenting a good buying opportunity. But the following table shows McDonald's (ticker symbol MCD) metrics; this is a great company, but a company whose stock performance exceeded its growth, which has since led to a correction.

TIME PERIOD	P/E RATIO	STOCK PERFORMANCE	EARNINGS GROWTH
Full year, 2010–2011	20	31 percent	11 percent
Quarter 1, 2011–2012	16	(14 percent)	5 percent

The first thing to do is to look at the first row of data. This information is from the full year 2010–2011 and takes into account the stock's growth year over year and then its stock performance from December 2010 until December 2011. Notice that the stock had gains of 31 percent despite earnings growth of only 11 percent. Sometimes this is okay, but only if the stock has a P/E ratio that is below its earnings growth. For example, if the stock's P/E ratio is 5, then it would be acceptable. However, its P/E ratio is nearly double its earnings growth, which means that the stock is growing much faster than its earnings. When this occurs and you see metrics such as this, you can be certain that the stock most likely will correct, unless the company all of a sudden begins growing by 30 percent year over year. And since McDonald's is a $90 billion restaurant, its chances of such aggressive growth are slim to none.

Now that you can see how overvalued shares of McDonald's were trading at the end of 2011, let's take a look at what happened next. In the first quarter of 2012, the adjustment period began to occur. The company's earnings grew by only 5 percent, and its

stock lost 14 percent of its value during the first six months of 2012. However, its P/E ratio is still 16 despite earnings growth of just 5 percent, which is probably consistent with its full-year earnings growth throughout the remainder of 2012. But since McDonald's is a massive multi-billion-dollar company that is well established and will continue to thrive, we have to consider a slight premium for its valuation because, after all, this is McDonald's that we're talking about. However, even with its 2012 loss, I still wouldn't buy nor would I consider the stock to be a value play. Most likely the stock will maintain a level of flat trading for the next 16 months until its metrics are more aligned. Some investors even may be tempted to buy because of its loss. Yet this is a perfect example that just because a stock falls doesn't mean that it is presenting value. Its growth is still nowhere near its valuation, and the distinction is simply too large for McDonald's to be considered a value investment.

If you determine that this formula is something you believe could be beneficial to your own strategy, then you need to identify extreme differentiations between value and growth (which is value investing). This strategy is yet another that can be incorporated using limits to find a cheap purchase price while eliminating emotion. I can tell just by looking at the earnings growth compared with performance and the P/E ratio that both Foot Locker and Apple are undervalued. There is a major misconception among investors that value is cheap, which means a stock only presents value when it is trading lower. However, this is simply not the case. A stock can easily trade flat for six months, yet it may grow by large margins and become a value if the company had a fair valuation at the start of the six-month period of flat trading. Similarly, a company can grow by 20 percent with a P/E ratio of 10 and stock gains of 5 percent and still be presenting upside and could be a good investment with further research. Whether you return gains or loss, it all depends on when you buy. This very simple formula can help you to determine whether a stock is presenting value. However, you must remember that this simple strategy is *one step*, not the *only* step in determining a buy. It just gives you a good start.

GREAT COMPANY, HORRIBLE STOCK

One of the more frustrating investments is the one that involves a great company but a horrible stock. In Chapter 7, I discussed short interest and short-interest ratios, and I indicated that when companies have high ratios using these metrics, they are often kept trading below their worth, regardless of fundamentals.

One of the most frustrating stocks I've ever owned is Spectrum Pharmaceuticals. I've owned it for several years and have returned very large gains, but the company constantly remains below its worth. It is one of the fastest-growing biotechnology companies in the market, and it has a diversified product line, a large pipeline, a lot of cash, and every positive indicator that you'd look for in a company. Yet it remains around $13 per share.

Perhaps the most significant reason that Spectrum trades with such an undervalued stock price is that it has high short interest and a high short-interest ratio. The stock is trendy, and once it reaches certain price levels, it trades lower aggressively. Over the last few years, it has had several periods where it would rally and reach new highs, but then it falls and trades to a lower level, although higher than previous lows. As a result, it is always trading in an uptrend, but the trend itself is very frustrating because this is a stock that should be trading at two to three times its current valuation.

Now here is where you test your patience as an opportunistic value investor, with companies such as Spectrum Pharmaceuticals. What is the correct way to play a company with sales growth of 50 percent, earnings growth of 90 percent, and a P/E ratio of under 8? Also, keep in mind that the company has a great balance sheet and strong cash flow to complement its fundamental growth. Your gut tells you to buy the stock, but because of its performance, you hesitate and may even start to believe that it's a deadbeat investment, which means that you believe it won't trade higher.

There are many stocks such as Spectrum in the market. Spectrum is a biotechnology company, and this particular industry is driven by speculation, rumors, and perception, unlike any other in the space. Therefore, in biotechnology, you have a large distinction in value, with some companies overvalued and others undervalued. But the good news is that even in an industry such as biotechnology, eventually a company's fundamentals and its valuation will align— but it may take some time.

In Chapter 9, I talked about Sprint and used it to explain how performance changes perception. When a stock falls, there are more investors who are pessimistic, but when it trades higher, all are optimistic. As an investor, if you expect to succeed, you need to change this thought process and be greedy when others are scared and scared when others are greedy. Companies such as Spectrum at $13 with a $780 million market capitalization or Sprint with a price under $2.50 and a market cap of $7.5 billion will eventually rise. These companies, and many more, have seen too great fundamental improvements to be kept down long term, and almost always when a stock falls in the category of "great company, horrible stock," once it starts to rise, the rise is very quick and very aggressive. Therefore, those who endure the volatility and frustrating returns are almost always rewarded with large gains.

CYCLIC VERSUS SECULAR

Perhaps the best indicator of which stocks to buy and when to buy should be the economy. Now keep in mind that I didn't say the market—I said the *economy*. Sometimes the market will trade higher despite slowed growth and a horrible economic outlook, and at other times it will trade lower despite improvements in the economy. A good example may be the auto stocks in 2011 and in the first quarter of 2012. Both Ford and General Motors have continued to create new lows despite being two of the true bright spots in the economy (a major sign that both stocks will rise).

Throughout this book I've told you to simplify the market and to try not to learn everything about all the companies that trade in the market but rather focus on certain industries or certain stocks and then broaden your knowledge over the course of years. However, one other way to break down the market and make it smaller is to monitor cyclic and secular companies by the strength of the economy. Allow me to explain.

A cyclic company will grow with a strong economy. It needs good growth and strong demand, and when these two catalysts are present, these stocks will flourish. These are companies that produce products that grow in demand when the economy is strong, such as steel and chemicals and, in some ways, the automotive and banking industries.

A secular company, on the other hand, does not need a strong economy to grow. It will perform well regardless of the economy. In fact, such companies tend to thrive in flat or even down economies. The reason is that secular companies create products that we must use, and when threatened in a down economy, investors will transition their money into these stocks as a form of protection against the down economy. Examples of industries in the secular space include food, dishwashing detergent and household necessities, biotechnology, medicine, and the less healthy tobacco and alcohol companies.

So how do you play secular and cyclic? A good way to play these trends and invest on the strength of the economy is to break the market into two sections, secular and cyclic. If the economy is thriving, then invest heavily in undervalued cyclic industries and/or companies. But when the market is flat or struggling, then buy stocks in companies that produce medicines that must be used, such as for cancer or diabetes, or Phillip Morris and Anheuser-Busch because people have to take medicine and will smoke, drink, or both regardless of the economy. Once you learn how to identify the direction of the economy, combine it with knowledge of the undervalued stocks in the space, and your returns will increase by an incredible margin and you'll be one step ahead of everyone else.

CHAPTER 17

Unconventional Diversification

Wide diversification is only required when investors do
not understand what they are doing.

—WARREN BUFFETT

WHAT IS DIVERSIFICATION AND WHY IS IT SO IMPORTANT?

The idea of diversifying a portfolio has been around for a long time.
Yet, because of the volatility in the market, it is often referred to as a
"safe haven" and is no longer used by retail investors. I remember a
retail investor who once said to me, "Holding long is dead," following an article I wrote that discussed the benefits of long-term investing. Well, for the most part, holding long and diversification have
diminished as research materials have gotten better. The delivery of
information is instantaneous, and online brokerage firms encourage
active trading in order to cash in on various fees. As a result, there
are more and more investors who have become desperate traders who
believe that they can outsmart the market with an active strategy.

Analysts blame the retail investor's shift from diversification on several factors. Some believe that it is due to pressure from online brokerages, and others may argue that it is a result of a change in perception because investors have become more desperate after a decade-long flat market with two substantial bear markets. Regardless of why this shift has occurred, it is an investment strategy that few retail investors are disciplined enough to honor, and those who are disciplined enough choose to avoid their father's more conventional methods of diversification. In fact, it seems as though the only investors who still honor conventional diversification are those with institutional backgrounds, people such as Jim Cramer.

If you've ever watched the TV show *Mad Money*, you've probably seen the segment entitled, "Am I Diversified?" This show involves viewers who call and present their portfolio holdings and then ask Jim whether or not they are diversified. Jim then goes through their holdings and tells them whether or not they are diversified based on Jim's opinion of the choices of stocks and the variety of industries included. The theory is that being diversified can and will better protect an investor in the event of a market downtrend and allow for better returns over the course of many years.

Wells Fargo Senior Equity Strategist Scott Wren explains the concept of diversification versus the market downturn by saying, "The theory holds that if a portfolio includes a wide range of investments that tend to perform out of sync with one another, then when some investments decline, others should post smaller declines, and some might even generate gains."

Yet, if this strategy is so wise and so efficient, then it would make sense that all investors would remain diversified and consistent with their investments. Scott Wren may have provided the answer when adding, "The last market downturn caused many investors to reexamine the conventional wisdom, however. The financial crisis caused nearly all assets—including stocks in every sector of the economy, developed and emerging foreign markets, commodities, real estate, and even corporate and municipal bonds—to slide in unison during late 2008 and early 2009. As a result, even thoroughly diversified investment portfolios were likely to have suffered negative returns."

Bottom line: We thought we had a system that worked and was safe, but it let us down. As investors, we can handle a little loss, but when the loss is half our life savings, we become a little anxious (rightfully so) and abandon the "conventional" methods that Wall Street professionals have deemed to be the right way to invest. Therefore, the phrase "diversify to survive" has become "don't own just to own."

WHY IS CONVENTIONAL DIVERSIFICATION BECOMING LESS EFFECTIVE?

In theory, a diversified holding would consist of stocks, bonds, fixed-income holdings, commodities, hard assets, exchange-traded funds (EFTs), mutual funds, foreign stocks, and even cash (Figure 17.1). The most diversified investors own assets in all possible investments. As I mentioned in Part I of this book, most money managers aim to diversify their clients' portfolios with index investing, thus causing confusion to investors who have no idea what assets they own. For example, the percentage of your investments that is allocated to commodities may consist of a fund such as the DFA Commodity

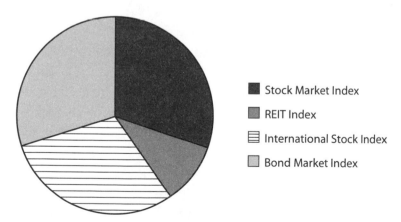

Figure 17.1   **Classic model of conventional diversification that involves a variety of investments.**

Strategy or other funds that are compiled of just Standard and Poor's 500 Index (S&P 500) stocks, so you always perform with the market. But considering the performance of the market, this strategy has not worked, and there is no reason to believe with certainty that this strategy will work anytime in the immediate future. Therefore, as Wall Street realizes this lack of performance, money managers are more frequently choosing foreign investments, and in some cases, investors may have as much as 40 percent diversified into foreign funds.

Prior to the new millennium, diversification was wildly successful because money managers could succeed by throwing money into just about any fund of diversified American companies. Take the S&P 500, for example; from 1980 until 2000, the index increased by over 1,200 percent, but it has since traded with a sizable loss. As a result, most investors have lost worth during the last 12 years. Honestly, it is no wonder that investors behave so irrationally and are now reluctant to embrace any level of diversification. First, we got spoiled with massive returns in the 1980s and 1990s, so we have become trained to expect the same returns. When they do not occur, we become desperate. Since we as humans have become a "what have you done for me lately" type of species, we have already forgotten the bull market before the 2000s and are now trying to develop a new strategy to capitalize from the trends of the market. Basically, humans evolve, and flat trading for more than a decade has changed our perception and forced us to evolve and avoid the common investment strategies that created wealth before the 2000s.

In the last 12 years, people like me have made a great deal of money by abandoning the more conventional methods of diversification and focusing on a new concept of diversification that takes into account the "new market." The "old market" was perfect for the conventional diversification strategy because it was always going up. In this new market, however, those who have maintained the same diversification strategies most likely have lost money since 2000. After all, it is hard to make money in a flat or slightly lower market if your goal is to invest in the entirety of the market. All you can do is perform with the market, which is a loss!

Most likely money managers will continue to operate with the same belief that equity markets will always rise and that conventional diversification will eventually pay off. To me, this belief sounds a bit ludicrous. Equity markets historically have traded higher, but is there any proof that they will continue to trade higher? All we have is past experience to gauge future performance. Over the last 12 years, a lot has changed, and we can draw several conclusions based on recent global struggles.

Eventually, investors must face the fact that U.S. equity markets may not trade higher for a long time. We may be stuck in this rut, and therefore, we have to evolve and learn how to trade in a volatile, flat market. If there is one thing we have learned from the last 12 years, it is that bear markets and recessions have several moving parts and are becoming more difficult to solve with each occurrence. When the United States is faced with economic struggles, they affect Europe too because of the connections in trade. When Europe is faced with similar problems, China may feel the burden, and because of constantly growing debt, the "problems" take longer to resolve and are more complex in nature.

If we consider that there are no guarantees that the market will trade higher, then how can we diversify our portfolios to succeed in a flat market? The first and most obvious step is to buy stock in fast-growing companies that are undervalued and have a plan on how to buy and sell the holdings (limit orders and expiration dates). More important, we can't just put all our eggs in one basket and bet our future retirement on one stock. Therefore, you must diversify your portfolio, but the question is how to diversify the portfolio if you are preparing for a flat market, and the old conventional methods of diversification no longer work.

REDEFINING DIVERSIFICATION FOR A FLAT MARKET

When you first started reading this book, I told you that I was going to challenge what you thought was right and present you with a number of new strategies to help you increase your return in a flat market. The process of redefining diversification is yet another process.

With traditional diversification, the goal is to invest in a little bit of everything. If you are investing in equity markets, you want to buy stocks in every sector along with owning assets in other investment categories. Although I agree with this concept, I do not agree with the concept of index investing, which is what diversification has become. The market with so much uncertainty has become driven by speculation. After 12 years of proof, I don't believe we can simply sit back and invest in the S&P 500 Index and rest assured that it will trade higher because it has in the past. Instead, I believe that we must diversify according to value and never mind the diversification of sectors, but rather we should be opportunistic and invest with a specific purpose, with each holding serving that purpose within your portfolio. To better explain this, allow me to describe my investment strategy as far as holdings are concerned and how I diversify my portfolio.

First, let me break down the conventional portfolio that you may see with a typical money manager. Remember, money managers chase indexes, so very rarely are you invested into individual stocks. Rather, they invest in a collection of indexes that are compiled of securities. Here's an example of a four-fund portfolio, although the number of funds held can get quite high. This one is courtesy of obliviousinvestor.com and was one of the more common portfolios that I have seen.

As you can see in Figure 17.2, the investor who is invested with this particular strategy is balanced into what appears to be a very safe and well-diversified portfolio. Looking at this figure may cause some investors to feel more comfortable with inflation-protected securities or even small-cap indexes, and you may wonder why I have a problem with this traditional diversified portfolio. Honestly, I don't have a problem with this style. However, it is very likely that you have returned no gains over the last 12 years in the stock market index. REITs are real estate investment trusts, so you can do the math, and depending on which international stock indexes you hold, you may be in a world of hurt. The returns from bonds would

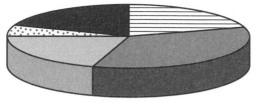

Long-Term Yield: 20%
Value Growth: 35%
Small Cap Value: 20%
Emerging Market Value: 5%
Cash/Bond: 20%

Figure 17.2   **Unconventional model of diversification, a model of choosing investments that serve a purpose rather than owning a broad range just to own it.**
Source: obliviousinvestor.com

barely make any difference, but it is still worth owning some for the sense of security.

The beauty of a diversified portfolio is that its beauty is in the eye of the beholder. Therefore, it is much like everything else in investing—no right or wrong. However, as a value investor, it seems almost wrong to invest in these large indexes because you get both the good and bad, so why not diversify with individual choices that present the characteristics of a value investment? Some people do invest in this manner, but those who do still make sure to include individual stocks from each sector because they have been trained to believe that this will create safety over the long term. I personally could care less if I own a stock in each sector. I only care that I am buying the cheapest stocks in terms of fundamentals and that I have a well-thought-out plan with each stock that is in my portfolio.

My goal when I am diversifying my portfolio is not to worry about or even consider the number of industries included but rather to buy stocks that serve a particular purpose within the portfolio. For example, I still provide myself with a balanced supply of yield, value, emerging markets, cash, and bonds, but I do not use index investing for the mere fact that I would be getting the bad with the good and would be relying on the law of averages for proof that the market will rise instead of investing in companies that are presenting value compared with fundamentals. So my strategy over many years has been to buy stocks that fit in each category of Figure 17.2, and then I sell once the stocks within each category appreciate. Simple enough?

Long-Term Yield

This section of my portfolio makes up 20 percent of my holdings, and its sole purpose is to provide returns in dividends. I use the same value-seeking strategy that I use with all my investments. I make sure the company is growing at a moderate rate, has a low valuation compared with growth, and is a company with a long-standing history of success. For this particular section, I like companies that are dominant but still have room to grow. Even though my only expectation is dividend return, I still set limit orders to profit if a stock reaches a certain price.

In theory, I usually hold between two and four stocks that fall in this category, which means that each position is somewhat large. I typically purchase stocks that trade in tight ranges with very modest 5- to 10-year gains, and my limit order to buy is always near the lowest point of the stock's 5-year range. I will wait and then buy, which means that I am able to capitalize not only on dividends but also when the stock returns to the top part of its range. As long as the company is growing, this strategy allows me to purchase very cheap and to sell fairly high.

For example, I just recently purchased BHP Billiton (BHP) at $60 per share. After looking at its chart, I saw that the stock has traded in a five-year range between $60 and $80 per share with one period where it traded up to $100, and during the recession, it fell to $30. Yet the stock tends to trade in this range, so I have had a limit order to buy at $60 for the last two months. The company has posted three years of strong top (revenue) and bottom (earnings) growth and has a strong balance sheet to complement its fundamental progress. But because of questions surrounding the materials sector, the stock has slipped to the bottom of its range. After my purchase, I immediately placed another limit order to sell the stock once it reached $90. I used $90 because that was above the stock's typical range, and if you incorporate fundamental growth, then the stock still would be undervalued at $90 if it maintains the same level of growth. Therefore, I believe that it is very possible for it to exceed this level.

The good thing about this investment is that I can still capitalize on the 3.5 percent dividend yield that the company returns to its investors. If it takes two years for the stock to reach the top of its range and hit $90, then I will return nearly 60 percent from the investment (counting the dividend). If it does not reach this level, then I still get to profit from the consistent dividend that has continuously increased over the last few years. Therefore, since I bought a growing company at the bottom of its range, it will most likely be a win-win situation for me. Other stocks I have recently owned for long-term yield are Johnson & Johnson (JNJ), Exxon (XOM), Coca-Cola (KO), Microsoft (MSFT), and Chevron (CVX).

Value/Growth

The value/growth portion of my portfolio is the largest and is a well-diversified portion. I use the tools that I have described in this book to find fundamentally fast-growing companies that are priced well below worth and then purchase the stocks when they are trading near the bottom level. This is where the aggressive growth under-valued biotechnology space investments are accumulated, along with any company that is growing quickly but is unrealized.

Small-Cap Value

I have always been a big fan of small-cap value stocks and use this section of my portfolio to invest in developmental biotechnology companies and other companies with major catalysts for future growth. I typically search for companies with unmeasured fundamental catalysts or developments that are company-changing in terms of growth. The amount I use per investment varies. With developmental biotechnology stocks, I usually buy between $3,000 and $6,000 in shares, but with companies in other industries I may initiate a much larger position. In 2012, the small- and midcap stocks moved the least in terms of positive performance during the first few months; therefore, I believe that this class of investments presents great opportunity.

Emerging Markets

As an investor, I don't like foreign index funds. I've never been a big fan of companies I don't know, and with the global economy facing so many challenges, I think this could be a dangerous space. Therefore, I invest very little in foreign companies and only when opportunity is evident. There are some money managers who focus only on foreign investments, and almost all money managers want to invest large positions in the prospects of foreign growth. My strategy includes choosing one or two foreign companies that also sell products or services in the United States.

Sodastream is a company with a very large presence in the United States but with headquarters in Israel. It is one of two companies I own with headquarters outside the United States The other is Alcatel-Lucent, a stock I purchased at $1.50 per share. Since August 2011, Sodastream has lost 50 percent of its value despite growing by 50 percent and showing earnings growth by 70 percent year over year, which means improved margins. The company also has significantly added to the number of stores that carry its products to over 10,000 and has recently announced several partnerships. However, some investors believe that its products are a fad and will be unable to stand the test of time. When I purchased the stock, it was trading with a price/earnings (P/E) ratio under 20; and if you consider its growth, the stock is very cheap. In fact, if the stock were to stay at its current price, then it would have a P/E ratio of under 13 next year, according to analyst expectations for future earnings growth. Therefore, a position in the company makes sense and is yet another stock with upside potential of more than 50 percent in a market that may very well trade flat over the next five years.

Cash/Bonds

People have often asked me how I have the discipline to wait so long before purchasing a stock. I usually respond by saying, "How do you not have the discipline?" I believe that having a strategy that involves a large cash position is king in determining how you will respond to market volatility and opportunity when it presents itself. There are some people who cannot stand to have cash positions because they feel as though they are losing or missing potential investments not owning a stock. People often become delusional and believe that when a stock rises, they "missed it" because they were going to buy it. Perhaps this is one reason that as retail investors we have such a tendency to buy when the market is trading higher versus being opportunistic and buying when it's lower.

By keeping a large cash position, I am able to keep my limit orders open and ready to execute. If you decide to attempt the limit strategy that I have discussed, then you must have cash to cover the trades at all times. Besides, keeping cash is good because you never know when a good opportunity will present itself.

I also use this section of my portfolio for bonds. However, I have never been a big fan of Treasury bonds or bills. Bonds are a very safe investment. My preference is municipal bonds because of the tax benefits associated with buying the bonds of your local government. If you are a person of wealth, it is always a good idea to invest in bonds that may provide additional returns, although not a direct return.

ONE SIZE DOES NOT FIT ALL

The most successful investors are able to keep a somewhat loose belief system and understand that conditions within the market can change overnight. They understand that the only way to experience long-term, sustainable success is to evolve and change with time. Hopefully, as you get older and more experienced, your wealth will grow larger, and your goals of investing will change.

I am sure that not all money managers feel the same, but those whom I have interviewed or spoken with over the last 10 years believe that the perfect portfolio is diversified between 5 and 7 percent of a person's total holdings in one stock. For those who use the index investing approach, a typical investor may own anywhere from two to eight funds, maybe more.

I personally have no problem with the idea of diversifying a portfolio with all industries, sectors, and a variety of investment types. I think that in a bull market this strategy works and has been proven to work with great success. However, in this flat market that could continue for many years, I feel that it is wiser to focus on value and stocks that fall for unexplainable reasons and then diversify your portfolio with stocks that serve a particular purpose.

How you choose to diversify your portfolio is a decision that you alone must make. But just because stocks historically have trended higher doesn't mean they will always continue to do so. I feel confident in saying that there is no such thing as a one-system-fits-all method to success in the market. You must continue to change with time and better protect yourself from risk as your wealth grows larger and your age grows older. When you first start and have $10,000, you may be more willing to accept risk for the possibility of reward. As you grow older, risk must be more averted, and your goals are consistency and preservation.

I just showed you the current way that I diversify my portfolio, but I must admit that it wasn't always balanced. Obviously, I prefer equity markets over other investments, but in the future I may turn more to real estate. If you attempt to invest with a system similar to the one I have discussed, then you should know that it doesn't have to look like mine. You can change as your goals change and you become wealthier. If you want to take more chances, then perhaps you should limit the yield or cash and invest primarily in undervalued/growth stocks. Also, change the number of stocks you own as your portfolio's value grows larger. If you are starting with $10,000, then it makes sense to only own two or three stocks because the likelihood for larger returns would be greater than if you owned 10 because the purpose of diversification is balance. If your portfolio grows and is worth $1 million, then it makes sense to diversify the portfolio to be better protected with possibly 25 holdings.

In the end, my process of diversifying a portfolio is nothing more than my way of hoping for a bull market but preparing for a flat market. With the problems in Europe, China's growth slowing, and unemployment still pathetic, there is no reason to believe that the market will trade considerably higher at any point in the near future. However, some investors are still stuck in the process of diversifying their portfolios with the belief that equity markets will rise, and others have given up on diversification and have moved to desperation and trend chasing. I believe that it is best to seek value in companies that are still growing and fundamentally outperforming the market. If you can buy these stocks cheap and are patient enough to wait, then you can capitalize on gains while index investors and sector investors remain at even and just waiting for the next bull market to occur. My theory is that a watched pot never boils, so why bother when there is so much value being created by the inconsistencies and irrational tendencies of the market.

CHAPTER 18

Success in a New Era

An investment in knowledge always pays the best interest.

—BENJAMIN FRANKLIN

TWO ERAS

The current state of the market is a tale of two eras that consequently involve two generations. Some may say that the dot-com bubble and the crash in 2008 killed the old and created opportunity for the new. It is a sad situation for the older generation who was near retirement but now has had to postpone retirement or be forced into a less than expected quality of life because of a crash that occurred near the end of their working careers. On the contrary, for those like me, the crash has created opportunity and a market marked with fear, which has created value in many fast-growing companies.

During the 20 years prior to the year 2000, the Standard and Poor's 500 Index (S&P 500) traded with gains of more than 1,200 percent. With gains like that, it is easy to see why investors believed that the best strategy was to buy index funds and then sit back and get rich. Since January 2000, though, the S&P 500 has been trading at a considerable loss, more than 8 percent as of today. As a result, it is just as easy to understand why some investors now believe that the buy-and-hold strategy is dead. However, the gains prior to 2000 were so large that even after the dot-com bubble burst and the financial meltdown, the S&P 500 still has had an annualized return of more than 8 percent over the last 20 years. This is incredible, but because of the assumed strength in financials, investors were heavily invested into the sector during the recession, like my friend Tara at the beginning of this book. Therefore, despite a positive annualized return since 1980, some investors still lost wealth because no one was prepared for the financial sector meltdown.

We now have two different types of investors. First, there are those who invested in the bull market prior to 2000, and then we have the new generation that has invested in the flat market since 2000. Personally, I fall into the second category, which causes me to look at the market in a different way than those who accumulated the majority of their wealth prior to 2000.

One of my favorite books was written by Mark Hebner, *Index Funds: The 12-Step Program for Active Investors*. The book is interesting because it is written as an intervention of sorts—to pull investors from an active strategy to a completely passive strategy of investing long term in more diversified holdings such as Treasuries and index funds. It shows that during the 20-year period between 1986 and 2005, the annualized return before inflation for the average equity investor was just 3.90 percent versus 11.93 percent for the S&P 500. This type of education about investing is what most have been taught to believe, and back during that era, this strategy was successful. Even before the recession, investors expected the market to return to normal, seeing as how we were in a 20-year bull market. But now this is simply not the case, and this new way of identifying value and profiting from inconsistencies by being aggressive yet passive isn't only new, but it is also unpopular among the "professionals" in the industry. The reason is simple: Most of the wealthy professionals today made their money in the bull market era and stay true to what made them wealthy.

Those of us who are of the flat market era are a product of our own unstable environment and now consider the performance of the market to be normal. We did not have the luxury of investing in a market with such large gains over a 20-year period. At this rate, we should just hope that over the next two decades our markets trade flat. This simply means that those of us who have experienced success have had to change our habits and become somewhat defiant toward all the books and other professionals telling us to invest solely in index and mutual funds. We have had to invest in a less conventional manner than those who were fortunate enough to reap the benefits of the 20-year bull market. Mark Hebner's twelve-step program makes sense and would have been a great intervention if the market would have returned to its bullish form. Without having any proof that the market will trade higher, though, after more than a decade of flat trading, I believe what is most obvious and what appears to be the most effective investment strategy in this new era, which is to buy a stock that is undervalued, hold onto it until it appreciates, and then sell it.

FROM BEVERLY HILLS TO EAST ST. LOUIS

The principles that I have enumerated in this book come from the eyes and experiences of someone who has been successful and accumulated wealth in the new era of flat trading. I am a classic example of someone who can't reminisce about or remember how easy it was to make money in the market prior to the dot-com bubble. If you have grown accustomed to the bull market era, then I imagine the last 12 years must have been one giant reality shock. During the bull market era, you could simply throw money in an index, sit back, and watch it grow year after year after year.

As we inch closer to the end of this book, it is necessary to put into perspective the mind-set of the market and the different thought processes of the two groups based on their experiences. Those who made money in the bull market continue to invest in index funds or diversify their portfolio with every industry in the hope that the market will trade higher. These people are actually just holding on for dear life and praying that the market returns to its glory years. Their behavior is normal and even praised by the investment professionals who also created the majority of their wealth during the bull market era. Since we don't know which direction the market will trade, it is very possible that the index fund bulls are correct, but then again, those who follow the principles of a value investor will be prepared as well, seeing as how we own nothing but cheap, undervalued stocks.

When we stop and look at the current state of the market and compare it with the bull market era, we might as well be comparing apples to oranges, Democrats to Republicans, or liberals to conservatives. In fact, there are no similarities. In the 20-year bull market, approximately 10 of the 20 years posted growth of more than 20 percent. However, in the new flat market era, we've only seen two years of 20 percent or higher growth, and those two years followed the dot-com bust and the recession, which provided no sense of growth to the economy.

Sometimes I don't think investors of my era stop to realize how fortunate we are to have started investing in the new millennium. Investors of the bull market have had to adapt to the changes in this new market, which is like living in Beverly Hills and then being forced to move to East St. Louis. Needless to say, the adjustment period would be quite dramatic. However, if you were born in East St. Louis, then you consider it to be the norm, having learned not only how to survive but also to be prosperous despite your surroundings. As silly as this may sound, this scenario is evident in all segments of the market because both investors and companies have had to change and adapt to their new surroundings.

DON'T PLAY IT BY EAR

In Chapter 2, I talked about the evolving marketplace and a company's inclination to change in order to survive. Smart companies were able to foresee the problems of the recession and identify how they were affected so that they could make changes that would protect their future. Unfortunately, these changes included a drastic cut in costs, a record amount of cash on balance sheets, and an apprehension on the part of the company to hire a larger workforce. These decisions have created anger among the general public, hence the Occupy Wall Street crowd. After all, who can imagine why a company with $5 billion in cash on its balance sheet wouldn't help the economy and hire new employees?

Large corporations are now better prepared to handle whatever the market decides to present. If for some reason Europe were to force the United States into another recession, large and even small corporations are now better equipped to deal with the burdens of a weak economy. With that being said, you must ask yourself how prepared you and your portfolio are to handle the burdens of an uncertain, potentially flat, or possibly a negatively driven economy. What are you doing to better prepare yourself for the next decade in the market?

Perhaps it is my experience as a counselor, or maybe I'm just a product of my own environment, but I think the best way to prepare yourself for what could happen next is to have a solid plan of action. All too often retail investors enter the market with a "play it by ear" strategy and end up losing significant worth. My belief is that the reason this occurs is because these people don't have a plan. They are simply waiting to see how the market opens and which stocks are trading higher/lower or what investments can return quick gains. Why? Because these people have no real plan.

I have often told new investors to approach the market and investing as they would an interview. Once again, this probably relates to my experience as a counselor because one of my primary job duties was to help clients with employment and teach them how to prepare for an interview. In the stock market, you want to be prepared anytime you are deciding on an investment, while always putting your best foot forward. This includes doing research and learning as much as you can about the potential investment or the potential job as possible.

Anytime you interview for a job you really want or one that could potentially change your life, you want to dot all your *i*'s and cross all your *t*'s. Even though you are 100 percent prepared and feel completely knowledgeable about the situation, there is still a chance that you won't get the job. However, you must always keep your head up; you can't just give up. You may have wanted the job very badly, and you may have spent hours in preparation, but sometimes the disappointment can be used as a learning experience. It may even force you to tune your skills toward something you will use later on down the road.

Regardless of whether or not you got the job, you still have a better chance of success when you are simply well prepared. If you go into an interview unprepared, then you are going to embarrass yourself and waste both your time and the time of your interviewer. Now let's compare this same situation to investing. You wake up one morning, check the Nasdaq for the morning's premarket movers, and then buy the stock, hoping that you can hold it throughout the day as it trades higher. This behavior, however, does not teach you anything. You might even be successful at first, but all it does is create an addiction and an investment strategy that becomes gambling. Instead, be prepared, do your homework, and even if you fail and the stock trades lower, you can use this as a learning experience. There may be times when all the *i*'s are dotted and the *t*'s are crossed, but you will still fail. It's how you respond to disappointment and failure and how well you honor your investment strategy that will create wealth over the long term.

CONCLUSION

Throughout this book I have made several suggestions, explained fundamentals in a way that I believe to be simple, and given you an inside look into some of the most common behavioral traps we as investors encounter on a daily basis. Despite this information and even my own success, I have always remained very open to the idea that you should have your own investment strategy. If you want to incorporate my ideas into your strategy, then I am confident they will improve your gains. The only strategy that I have said you must do in order to improve your gains and control your emotions is to document all your investments. This would include writing down the prices you bought/sold, reasons why you bought or sold, what you noticed about the stock's performance, and any other thoughts about the investment. Conclude in your notes what you learned from the experience; this will help you to make better decisions in the future.

I hope that by reading this book you are now more open to change and will be able to embrace a new market that is filled with value but also uncertainty. I also hope that today starts a new era for you as an individual investor, whether you have never purchased a stock or you are a 30-year veteran. The fact of the matter is we are now investing in a new market. If you have been unsuccessful, it is most likely due to common mistakes that many investors find themselves making in an attempt to either regain from a loss or make money as quickly and easily as possible. I encourage you now to enter the marketplace with a new and adjusted investment strategy that has been conditioned to make money in a flat market. By preparing to make money in a flat market, you will be pleasantly surprised if and when the market enters another bull era. The fact of the matter is that the market is undervalued, more so than at any period of the last 13 years. But the first step toward success in an uncertain market, once you have created a new adjusted strategy, is to have a plan of action so that you are well equipped for whatever happens next.

Ask yourself these questions:

- What are your short-term goals?
- What are your long-term goals?
- How much risk are you willing to take?
- How much of your portfolio should return yield (dividends)?
- Which of your personality traits could become a liability?
- What parts of a company's fundamentals are most important to your research goals?

- Which unmeasured fundamentals are most important to you?
- How are you going to ensure that you are buying a stock when it presents value?
- What is most important when choosing an online brokerage firm?
- Do you have a good exit strategy?

Now write down the answers to these questions. Use the answers to help guide you in this wacky and unpredictable market. You already know how to identify value, you understand fundamentals, and you are conscious of the basic mistakes of investors. Now use this information to your advantage. Don't be your own worst enemy. Give yourself the opportunity to learn from your mistakes, and if you don't like the answer to one of the questions, then change your behavior. Don't make investing more difficult than it has to be. Develop a great plan, and you will succeed in this new era of investing.

Index

About the Author

Brian Nichols is a well-known financial writer whose name began to circulate among the investment community in 2011. His strategy of using the behavior of the market along with the principles of value investing provided a very large following, as the number of people who flocked to read and understand his strategies and opinions have exceeded 3,000,000.

Unlike money managers who earned wealth by managing other's money and collecting large commission fees, Brian Nichols has achieved wealth as an individual investor, in a flat market. Brian Nichols' perspective is written solely from someone who has experienced success in a flat market, who does not entertain stories of the bull market in the 1980's or 1990's. Readers can easily relate to Brian, as he relates to the average investor who is trying to make money in a market that is designed to make the rich richer while taking from the little guy.

Before becoming a professional investor Brian worked as a counselor for the Department of Corrections, helping those incarcerated prepare for life outside of prison. The tools he developed in this position have helped to form his investment strategy. As he often compares teaching an investor to change their bad habits to teaching a career criminal to live a crime free life. Brian's psychological principals revolve around similar ideas that have led him and many to achieve wealth in a flat and unstable market.